ROBBERS ROOST RECOLLECTIONS

Cabin built in 1915 by my father when my mother refused to go back to Hanskville for the winter. Photo by Hal Lynde, 1989.

The first granary built to protect grain (oats and corn) fed to the horses and to store other supplies and equipment. Photo by Hal Lynde, 1989.

ROBBERS ROOST RECOLLECTIONS

PEARL BAKER

Utah State University Press
Logan, Utah
1991

Other Titles in the Western Experience Series

Cattle in the Cold Desert
James A. Young and B. Abbott Sparks

The Roll Away Saloon: Cowboy Tales of the Arizona Strip
Rowland Rider as told to Dierdre Paulsen

Wild Mustangs
Parley J. Paskett

Heaven on Horseback
Austin and Alta Fife

Copyright © Utah State University Press, 1976

Library of Congress Cataloging in Publication Data

Baker, Pearl Biddlecome.
    Robbers Roost recollections.

    1. Ranch life—Utah.   2. Baker, Pearl Biddlecome.
3. Utah—Biography.   I. Title.
F826.B169   979.2'03'0924   76-4915
ISBN 0-87421-083-6

To Joe and Millie Biddlecome's grandchildren:
My successful sons, Joe, Jack and Noel Baker;
and Hazel and Arthur Ekker's outstanding
children: Eddyjo, Evelyn (Tissy) Shaw, Gaye
Thurston and A.C. Ekker,

I dedicate this partial record of their unique heritage.

Contents

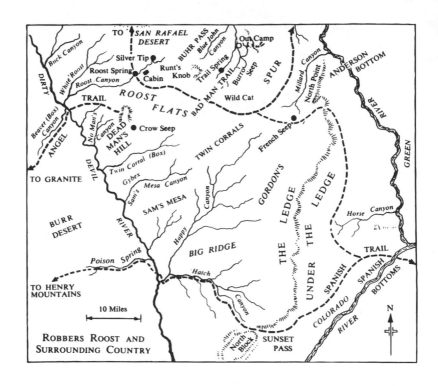

Robbers Roost and Surrounding Country

Map labels:

TO SAN RAFAEL DESERT

Buck Canyon
White Roost
Roost Canyon
DIRTY
TRAIL
Beaver (Box) Canyon
ANGEL
TO GRANITE
DEVIL
BURR DESERT
RIVER
Poison Spring
TO HENRY MOUNTAINS

BUHR PASS
Blue John Canyon
Out Camp
Silver Tip
Runt's Knob
Trail Spring
Cabin
Burro Seep
Wild Cat
SPUR
Millard Canyon
North Point
ANDERSON BOTTOM
GREEN RIVER
ROOST FLATS
BAD MAN TRAIL
No Man's Canyon
DEAD MAN'S HILL
Crow Seep
Twin Corral (Box)
Gybex
Sam's Mesa Canyon
SAM'S MESA
TWIN CORRALS
French Seep
GORDON'S SPUR
Happy Canyon
Canyon
Horse Canyon
THE LEDGE
UNDER THE LEDGE
BIG RIDGE
Hatch
Canyon
SPANISH
SPANISH
BOTTOMS
TRAIL
COLORADO RIVER
North Block
SUNSET PASS

10 Miles

N

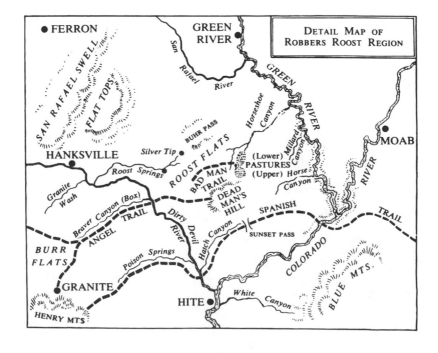

Detail Map of Robbers Roost Region

Map labels:

FERRON
GREEN RIVER
San Rafael River
SAN RAFAEL SWELL
FLAT TOPS
BUHR PASS
Silver Tip
ROOST FLATS
Horseshoe Canyon
GREEN RIVER
MOAB
HANKSVILLE
Roost Springs
Granite Wash
Beaver Canyon (Box)
ANGEL TRAIL
Dirty Devil River
BAD MAN TRAIL
(Lower) PASTURES
(Upper) Horse Canyon
DEAD MAN'S HILL
Millard Canyon
SPANISH
SUNSET PASS
TRAIL
COLORADO RIVER
BURR FLATS
Poison Springs
Hatch Canyon
BLUE MTS.
GRANITE
HITE
White Canyon
HENRY MTS.

1

Getting a Start

THERE WAS ONLY one reason my parents took their outfit to Robbers Roost—it was a last, desperate stand to make good in the cattle business; and my father, Joe Biddlecome, was a cowman. Once in a while a cowman comes along who will "lay out with his cows" and build a herd. I have known only three or four, and they were looked down on by their more lethargic neighbors as being cow thieves, and they found their activities curtailed by one method or another. Usually they spent a little time in jail, and then either moved or became a bit less ambitious.

The neighbors were not entirely wrong. An energetic man who is willing to camp around winter and summer, and in spite of great personal discomfort, take care of his herd, is enough of an opportunist to recognize his rightful calf, even if "the stupid little bastard is following a cow with someone else's brand on."

However, that is only a small part of the story. This herdsman carefully eases his cows through the winter, moving them to feed and shelter and therefore cutting his loss. His neighbors spend the bad weather with their feet in "Ma's oven," and cows get into cul-de-sacs, are snowed in and die of starvation before spring.

In the summer this good cowman mixes his cows and bulls together. He herds, drives and corrals them often, so that his calf crop zooms; his neighbor's bull runs with four or five cows all year, and sees the rest of his harem only at the water holes and probably at the wrong times. Good herdsmanship does pay off.

Joe Biddlecome grew up around Ferron, which lies in Castle Valley, Utah, then went to stay with an older half-brother, Alex Reid, in Castleton above Moab on the Colorado River. He worked for his brother a year or two, then struck out for himself, working around in eastern Utah and western Colorado on and near the La Sal Mountains. He took calves for wages, traded and acquired calves by other means (I am told), until he had accumulated a small herd by the time he married my mother, Millie Scharf, in 1904.

Together they set up their outfit on Piñon Mesa, that rough, broken high country running from the La Sals out to the Colorado River at the confluence of the Dolores and Colorado. Gateway, Colorado, lies on the southeastern flank of Piñon Mesa; the Utah Bottom, where my mother grew up, lies just over the line into Utah, around a point on the Dolores some ten miles or so above the confluence. Piñon Mesa covers some 400 square miles of heavily timbered, wild country of narrow ridges, high points and deep canyons, with very little open country.

A few years before, the S-Cross outfit had moved into the area, and had suffered the customary depredation of the local ranchers. All of the big outfits of the West were finally put out of business by just this same thievery; while many, many small outfits, some of which became important later, sprang up throughout the ranges. The S-Cross had not yet met this fate, but small outfits were springing up. When the big outfit had no more cattle to graze, it didn't have any range to run them on, either. There were no vested range rights, a man took his cattle and horses into a country and set up an outfit, and that is what my parents did on Piñon Mesa.

Joe Biddlecome had a rare gift: he was always perfectly oriented. He never got lost, and he never lost anything on the range. Riding for his cattle on Piñon Mesa once, he watched from a high point as a couple of neighbors tied up two S-Cross calves, then drove the cows down the gully and shot them. This was standard procedure, but he considered it wasteful since those cows would likely produce calves again the next year.

After killing the cows, the fellows went back up another draw, instead of back to the calves, which puzzled Joe. They rode around some, never coming near the calves, then turned and went home.

The next morning Joe perched again on the point, not to watch developments particularly, this was none of his business, but just to look around generally. He had phenomenal eyesight and didn't need field glasses to see everything that would be of any interest to him. The fellows were back, riding around in circles, criss-crossing back and forth. They didn't go near the cows, but by the time they had made a couple of passes over the area, tracks were no longer a help to them, but a hindrance.

Joe watched in amazement while they completely "rode out" a canyon off to one side of the one where the calves were tied in a cedar copse. Then they moved over into that canyon, rode back and forth across it until well up past where the calves were, missing them by yards as they rode past the clump of cedars.

About this time it dawned on him that they had lost the calves. He dropped down off the point, gathered in the calves and, necking them together, drove them home to his own milk cow. If the boys came along and recognized them, what could they say?

All his life Joe Biddlecome had a blacksmith shop. He liked to work with metal, and his profession required tools that he could make cheaper than the ones he could buy, and he loved to do it. He was always most creative, usually with material at hand. As soon as he had built a one-room log cabin on Piñon Mesa, he set up a simple shop where he made bridle bits, spurs, branding irons and other tools of his trade, as well as shod horses, which was a necessity in the sharp rocks of the La Sal mountains. Passersby often stopped and talked a while, then rode on.

Mama tells about one fellow who stopped at the shop and asked, "What do you think of my new horse, Joe?" My father didn't even look up from the horseshoe he was shaping, but said the horse was all right—still a little "wet," but a good animal. My mother was amazed; the horse was not even sweaty—she didn't know that this referred to the brand which had been "worked" so recently that it was not yet healed, but that fact had not escaped my father's expert eye.

One day in early fall three of the leading cattlemen of Gateway rode up to his camp and found him at the forge. He was alone; Millie was down on the Dolores at the Utah Bottom visiting her folks. Joe laid aside his work, a spur he was roughing out, and invited them to step down and go up to the cabin for dinner.

"No, Joe, we just want to talk to you," the leader said.

"Talk." He banked the fire in his crude forge and turned his attention to them.

"Well, Joe it's like this," the leader seemed to be making heavy work of his errand, and he was getting little help from his committee. "We like you fine—"

"Good. Like you fellows, too." Joe swept his hat back to

enjoy the afternoon breeze on his white, untanned forehead, while he built and lighted a Duke's Mixture cigarette. "So?"

Not because he was the tallest man there, six feet two inches, or because he was the smartest or the best-looking of the group, but just because he had a kingly bearing and masterful air, he plainly was the dominant figure. The spokesman hesitated, looked at one of the men with him, who gestured with his thumb to go ahead.

"Well, Joe, you're a good cowman—"

"Try to be."

"Well, you are, and now you've got a little bunch of cows. But we figger the range is all took up hereabouts. There just ain't room for another outfit."

"Don't feel crowded at all."

"Well, by God, Joe, we do." The older of the fellows spoke up. He was a grizzled old cowman, twisted and scrawny, with the mark of many hard rides on his wasted body, while his blue eyes looked out through wrinkles of many suns. "I told Bill here we wouldn't find you easy to handle, and that's why I come along. I like you, and I like your brother Alex, and I don't want to see you get into trouble."

"Just how am I going to get into trouble?" Joe looked up at him sidewise under his eyebrows. "I can handle quite a bit of that."

"I know you can," the old man spoke ruefully. "And if I was a younger man, you'd sure be a challenge, but I'm too old to range war anymore, and I don't want my son to have to learn." He dropped his hand on the young fellow's shoulder. "So why don't you just pull up stakes and move on."

"With a hundred and twenty-five head of cattle? Where the hell to? All the best range is taken and us young fellows have to take what's left out on the fringes. I just don't plan to do that. Since the S-Cross is about gone, there's room for another outfit here and it's gonna be mine."

"No, it ain't." Bill put in his oar again. "We'll take care of all the extra range as time goes along."

"Like hell you will." Joe's temper was always on low boil with fellows like these. "You birds set on your tails on your little ranches down on the rivers and let your cows take care of themselves. Me, I take care of mine."

"And some of ours, too—so they say," Bill added hastily as the big man took a step toward him.

"Now, Joe," the older man spoke kindly but firmly, "don't get mad. We are trying to tell you something. We like you fine, but we—just—can't—afford—you. That's right, Bill?" He turned to let Joe think a few seconds.

"That's right." Bill slapped his palm with the ends of his bridle reins. "We just can't go through another calf season with you on the range. Think it over, Joe. You're going, one way or another." And without another word they mounted and rode away.

Joe yanked his hat low and stood with his head down, hearing the horses' hoofs click on a rock now and then in the steep mountain trail. The message was clear—loud and clear. If he stayed he'd go to jail or wind up dead in the bottom of a hidden gully. He had to move. Thoughtfully he went back to the forge and worked the bellows to bring up his fire again.

The next morning he started gathering his cattle, pushing his "hold" into a canyon he had been saving for winter. He wouldn't need that now.

When Millie and the baby came back from her folks', he told her the ultimatum and sent her back with word for her brother, Offie Scharf, to be ready to help him trail his herd to the San Rafael desert for the winter. In the spring he'd probably move on back to Castle Valley, or do whatever looked best at that time. Now, it was fall, and winter was his main concern.

A couple of weeks later he crossed the Colorado at Dewey,

and he and Offie trailed the small herd across the country to the Green river at Little Valley, where they forded the river. I have been told that he had about thirty head of grown cows, forty head of yearling heifers and about that many calves, not counting the eight head following the three milk cows. This was quite a calf crop, considering he had only two bulls, both yearlings.

As soon as he had his cows on feed south and west of Green River, he sent for his family. His father-in-law brought Millie and the baby, May, just past a year old, over in a wagon. They crossed the Colorado at Moab on the ferry, and ferried again at Green River.

He planned to settle his family in Green River, but that town was in the throes of the 1906 land boom, and there wasn't a house to rent. They pitched a tent down on the river bottom, intending to live there that winter. Little May died in November, and Millie was so shattered Joe couldn't leave her there alone. He had to stay with his cattle, so he moved the tent out to a little spring where they stayed that winter. His brother, Nate, and his family moved down for a while, too, living in another tent close by. This was called Biddlecome Spring (the only place that ever carried his name), but since that time, another family, the Smiths, moved their cattle into that area, and changed the name of the spring to "The Cow Camp."

Joe was reluctant to build a permanent camp. He didn't like the country, and neither did his cows. After a miserable winter, and a worse summer, he moved his cattle to the San Rafael desert country, where his old friends from Castle Valley were wintering their herds. I was born in that awful summer, 1907, but since all this is before my time, I prefer to tell it mostly in the third person.

Castle Valley runs from Emery on the south to Elmo on the north, with towns and farms along its streams. These farmers ranged their cattle on Ferron Mountain in the summer, but if they could find a suitable winter range, they could sell their hay, rather than feed it to their herds, thus making two incomes. The first year (1906-7) that they took cattle to the San Rafael desert through the Reef from Sinbad, the cattle had done well. The winter my father moved out there was long and bad, and the spring uncertain, with warm spells that made the water level in the San Rafael river fluctuate, increasing the loss in quicksand many-fold.

When the water level dropped, exposing bars and banks of quicksand, cows coming in for water had to wade out over these traps. Their sharp hoofs cut through the firmer sand on top, and sank down to where the sand was water-logged beneath. When they tried to pull out their legs, some of the water was forced out and the sand set up almost like concrete around their slim shins. They could no longer pull out a leg easily, and as they tried first one then another, they worked down until their bellies rested on top of the sand bank, and often deeper than that. There, if someone "riding bog" didn't find and extricate them, they died.

The drive in the spring of 1908 to the Ferron Mountain was one for the books: my mother and I rode in the chuckwagon with Charley Larson, who grieved because he could find neither feed nor water enough for his beloved team. The drive started too late, after the calves started coming, with numbers of them born on the trip. These young, tired calves dropped behind, often lying down behind a bush where they were not seen, with the ones discovered hauled or carried until they were rested enough to go on a bit farther. Cows dropped back, sure their calves had been left behind, and had to be forced along. There was no leader among the men, and therefore no order to any of the drive.

The days were hot and dry, and there was never enough water for either the animals or the men. A rider brought in a water bag of water he had found in a small rock tank in a gulch one day and passed it along. When it got to a fat kid, who had suffered more than most from the blazing sun, he took a drink, then upended the bag and poured the rest of the water down over himself. It was not a popular thing to do!

After reaching the mountain, Joe was miserable. His cattle weren't doing very well and he couldn't help them much. That fall the Castle Valley farmers put their cattle back on the farms, but there was no place else for Joe to go but back to the San Rafael, which he did. He built a small cabin on Harris Bottoms, where he settled his family while he rode with the cattle. But he knew this was only a stop-gap; in the spring he had to find range somewhere.

We lived in the tent, but under the crude saddle shed can be seen quarters of beef, hung out in the cold weather. Note the snow on the ground.

Breaking road with four-horse team and wagon, the only transportation we had for many years. My father driving.

2

The Trip to the Roost

JOE BIDDLECOME SIDESTEPPED the slashing horns of the cow he had just pulled out of the mud of the river bank, and, having held the end of her tail for just this contingency, gave it a yank and headed her across the saltgrass flat away from the river. She let out a "Blur-rt" of panic and staggered off through the cottonwoods.

Joe picked up his rope and started coiling it as he watched her. He hoped she was scared and mad enough to carry her bulk across the unpalatable salt-grass and into the highly nutritious fresh, spring sandgrass in the hills and draws bordering the river bottom. This was the third cow he had pulled out of the San Rafael mud while riding bog the last two days, and while she had not been in deeply, her calfy bulk made her hard to handle. He was wet above the knees and elbows, while the sticky blue river mud plastered his boots and spurs.

He had dug the cow's legs loose by hand, while she tried to hook him every time she got a chance. Then he had hitched his rope around her horns and dragged her around and out of the mud hole. As he had expected, she could not get on her feet, so he tailed her up; when she, again expectedly, tried to kill him, he handled her expertly.

Turning to his tired horse, he deftly buckled the rope into the rope-strap, slipped the tiefast over the horn and swung the trailing reins over his horse's head as he rounded to the left side. He hitched up his pants, caught his stirrup and stepped aboard. His muddy boot made a soggy chunk as it hit the metal stirrup he had shaped to his liking a few months before, at a neighbor's blacksmith shop. He turned his weary mount toward the sod-roofed log cabin he had built the fall before, where his wife and baby were waiting for him.

As he rode up the river bank at a trot, still riding bog, he wished desperately he knew what he was going to do. Up to two years ago he did—get a bunch of cows together. And when he had done it, by every means at the command of a young man of unusual intelligence, energy and ambition, he found his very talents had excluded him from the range on Piñon Mesa. He had to leave, but he hadn't bettered his situation much.

He recalled the trip to Ferron Mountain the spring before, and was glad he didn't have to face that again. And he remembered the summer when they never sat down to a meal alone. While he was openhanded and hospitable, the steady string of boys sent by their rancher fathers onto the mountain with no outfits had been more than his frugal larder could hold up under, and he determined to stay clear from now on. This set-up was no good either. When he had built his cabin the fall before, he was determined to run his cattle by themselves. While the small Gillies herd was no problem, riding bog was an almost year-round activity, and he still lost to the bog-holes.

When he came up to the cabin, Millie saw him and ran out with the baby. I was that baby, but this was before I counted much—let's keep it impersonal for a while. He dismounted and hugged them, then she went back to finish supper while he unsaddled and hobbled his horse in the sand draw near where the other three grazed. Millie had mentioned that these horses had been into water in the afternoon and had hopped back past the cabin, snatching at the sparse salt grass, but headed for better grazing.

The fried beef (nights were still cool enough to keep fresh beef by hanging it out at night and rolling it in a bedroll during the day) and beans tasted good to a man gone all day without a lunch. Afterward, telling Millie about his day and his worries about the future, they talked the matter over again. Gillies had never complained because they were still on the river with their cattle, but Joe felt that he was moving in on an established right, and he didn't think it was fair.

"I'm going to look at the Robbers Roost country," he said finally. "Em Wild has been out there with his cows, but it's over a hundred miles from home, and he's leaving."

"It'll be a hundred miles from your home any way you look at it, too," Millie pointed out as she got the babbling baby ready for bed. "I'm not for living in Ferron or Castle Dale or anywhere in Castle Valley, so the next place is Green River. I hate to go there, too," she said after a short pause, and they both remembered Little May.

"What about Hanksville? It's only about 45 miles from the Roost."

"That's so," she was thoughtful. She had heard of Hanksville, a little Mormon town on the Dirty Devil River. In Castle Valley she had found little to admire among the Mormons. To her their beliefs and customs were sheer superstition that bordered on witchcraft, and she had observed that often a man found his religion could be given a deft tweak and come out to his advantage. As near as she had been able to gather, this was common practice right up through the hierarchy to the leaders, who reinforced their tweaks with visions. To go back into that environment with her family coming on wasn't exactly her cup of tea.

"Anyway," he argued, "you can live at the Roost most of the year, just stay in town two or three months in the winter."

"What about school? It's only a few years until Pearl here will be old enough, and we may have more coming along."

"Well, what about school?" Joe yanked his boots off and took them outside to beat off the half-dried mud on the corner logs of the cabin. As he turned back to the door, he continued, "You can teach them to read and write and that's good enough." He bent to enter the low door. "More than I can do and I get along OK. All I need to read is brands."

He backed up in amazement and would have turned and escaped if he'd had any warning at all. Millie was standing in her nightgown in the middle of the floor, in the candle light. She was barely five feet two inches tall, but she looked as big as a locomotive to Joe, and fully as capable of running a man over.

"Joe Biddlecome, get one thing straight: You do whatever you have to with those cows to make a living, but when the time comes, our kids go to school. I got all the education I could, but I had to quit."

"Why, sure Tootsie." He had called her Tootsie in fun before, but after this he called her that all during their life together. She burst into tears and ran to him. They were both shaken; she had never in the years of their marriage stood up for her rights. Women just didn't in those days at the turn of the century. That night they lay long awake and talked, and cemented a strong marriage that lasted until Joe died many years later.

The next morning he packed a small outfit on Babe and saddled Browney to hunt a range where he could run his cows as he saw fit, with no interference. He was looking for isolation and Ern had told him the Roost had that. It was good range, but with no water except the Roost Spring and rain water in the round potholes of the canyons. These were veritable traps for cattle, Ern had said, and he was getting out while he could. This would leave the Roost "open," so Joe headed up Dugout Draw, leading the pack horse which would follow when he had put a few miles between him and home.

The seventh day he returned, and after greeting his family, turned out to graze horses that were too tired to do so. He had ridden them both into the ground, and although he was a big man, he was a superb rider and by his balance and moving with the horse instead of against it, could exact more from a mount than many a smaller man without these instinctive skills. He had covered a lot of territory.

"I've found it," he was almost too excited to eat. "I've found what I've been looking for—the best range left."

"What's it like?"

"Open swales and sand hills at the Roost, sloping up into a high cedar ridge. Beyond is an open high valley, different, richer, with grassy swales running up into the cedar and piñon ridges. Goes up into the sage in some places. Deep canyons break away on all sides, but they have good feed, too, and will be fine for holding weaners or to gather a trail bunch into."

"And the water?"

"Ern was about half right about that," he admitted. "But I think I can fix some of that. I know things Ern don't—I've mined. Some of the tanks I looked at can have trails blasted out of the sides where they aren't the cow-traps he lost to. While the springs as big as the Roost are in deep canyons, I found some small ones on top that can be developed to water a few head. The Roost needs some fixing, too, for that matter."

The next morning Joe rode into Green River with a letter to Millie's two brothers, Offie and Clyde Scharf on the Utah

Bottom to come and help him move. One of them could help him with the cattle, and the other could drive the wagon, making the trip easy for Millie and the baby.

He started to gather his cattle, pushing them up Dugout Draw. This was no pasture—they could and did drift back to the river, but he was riding the outside edges, and most of his stock now ranged on the ridges out of Dugout and watered back in the bitter water of the Draw. Shortly after the first of June, he had a letter from the Scharfs saying that maybe Offie could come over for a few days about the middle of the month, but Clyde was too busy to come. This irked him, he had been good to the kids, and he was so desperately in need of their help that it was hard to ask for it.

He rode up to the Gillies' ranch to see if he could hire a couple of the boys. Only Charl was on the ranch, and he was deep into spring work with haying crowding him and couldn't go.

This was only another challenge to the big cowboy. By God, Millie had ridden for the mail all her life on the Utah Bottom, and had even helped him before Little May was born. She could go along and, even carrying Pearl, keep the drags up while he pointed the herd and did most of the riding. He'd come back for the wagon later.

Millie didn't have a saddle, so he borrowed one from Charl, who apologized for its battered condition, but it was all he had. It was really just the saddle tree, most of the leather had weathered off, and there were no stirrups on it. Cinches Joe could make, and since all Millie needed was something to ride on and anchor a pillow for the baby to sit on, it would have to do.

Millie was appalled when he rode in and threw the saddle down, but there was no holding him. He had found a range and come what might, he meant to take it before someone else did.

He rode bog again the next day, but was so lucky he thought it was surely a sign. He rounded up the lower bottoms and turned his hold up Dugout. That evening he repaired the old saddle as best he could, and the next day rode up the river and brought one cow and calf back from there. He didn't think there were any across the river; he had pushed them all to the south side before high water.

The morning for departure found the horses in and saddled, breakfast over and Millie and the baby ready to go. Pearl was delighted. "Go horsey!" she kept piping in her almost two-year-old voice, "Go horsey!"

The pack carried only the bare essentials for a few days camping trip. Joe had suggested a few extra clothes for Millie and the baby, limiting the supplies to staples, with cooking equipment kept to a dutch oven, frying pan and coffee pot. The bed, Millie knew by experience, was going to furnish only the barest protection from the elements and none at all from the rocky ground.

She mounted, tucked a pillow into the front of the saddle, Joe handed the baby up to her and they started up Dugout. Millie rode the wash, hallooing the cattle ahead of her, as Joe rode both sides and shoved them in. In the late afternoon they camped and ate supper, which Joe fixed while she got the baby ready for bed. It had been a hard, long day in the hot sun and she was tired.

She and the baby were asleep before the June sun went down, but Joe was out with the cattle, bunching and settling them for the night. Long before daylight he had his "crew" up and on their horse. Just as it was light enough to see, he caught the first cows leaving the bedground, most of them headed back toward the river for a drink.

"They'll get a good deal dryer before they're through with this," he told Millie. "Dry camp at the gap on Black Ridge and tomorrow over and up to North Springs. I dug it out the other day, made some pools with an old shovel and if we hold there all night, I think I can water them all some. It's too far for the heavy cows and some of the little calves, too," he worried.

Millie thought privately it was too far for a tired woman and a small girl, too, but she didn't mention it. In fact, Joe was gone even before he finished his comment, and all morning she saw him only from a distance as he expertly handled his herd. He didn't plan for a cow to take a step except in the right direction, and few did. They traveled slowly and Millie kept special watch that a calf didn't stop and get left behind. There were only four or five small ones, and she kept back from them as Joe had told her to do, but every time they wanted to stop, she was there and they went on a bit farther.

The caravan paused for lunch, and went even slower in the afternoon. Topping the ridge at last, Millie could look south to where the black lines of the Roost country's cedared ridges showed faintly. It was far, she thought; this was sure a big country.

Joe maintained the same procedure again of settling the herd, but some of the cows giving milk were pretty dry and he rode most of the night.

There was no long stop for lunch this day, the cattle were too thirsty to graze. Millie mounted and fixed the pillow, but Pearl, when her father swung her up and hugged her, said, "No go horsey." But she was beyond a choice; it was too late to turn back now.

That afternoon Millie stopped for a brief rest and, parking Pearl on a sand bump, mounted and got the pillow stuffed in front of her in the old saddle. She reached down, but the baby shook her head and put her hands behind her, saying, "No go horsey." Millie reached as far as she dared, but her short legs gave her so little purchase she was afraid to lean too far and lose her balance. She was tired and hot; the cattle were getting farther and farther ahead. Using the snapping ends of the bridle reins as a persuader soon brought up the little hands where she could reach them, and she swung the baby up. Looking up, she saw her husband watching, but he didn't say a word. After that, he was around to help her more often.

When the cattle dropped over the banks into the gravel of North Springs wash, they gained speed in the better going, and Joe held back the leaders. When the sides of the wash led into low walls and bluffs, he dropped back and took the baby, saying for Millie to line out and beat the cows to the water holes in the head of the canyon and fill the water bags.

A change of pace felt good, she thought, as she touched up her mount and worked along the side of the herd. It was a great feeling of freedom not to have to hold the heavy baby, and she moved her aching arms and shoulders and smacked the pony with the ends of the bridle reins as she cleared the herd, and loped up the gravelly wash bottom.

Suddenly the canyon forked. Joe hadn't mentioned that. Turning left she spurred her mount into the fork and scattered gravel until the blank wall of the canyon head confronted her. She couldn't see any water and Joe had said there were several pools.

Turning she spurred her horse down the canyon on a dead run, but it was too late. The cows had smelled the water and were lining out into a trot and lope and she came in just behind Joe and the baby. He had ridden into the herd and jerked the lead-rope of the packhorse loose, and was also leading it.

Hearing her running horse, he looked around and couldn't believe his eyes. For a second he was furious; then he tossed in the towel. He hadn't mentioned the fork because it was such a small, obvious branch. To him, the main canyon was so clearly just that; he didn't think—he couldn't imagine— anyone's not seeing it, too.

He kissed her and handed the pillow then the baby back

and trotted up to make camp under a cottonwood tree in the canyon. Their camp would hold the herd on water all night, and by morning some of the cattle would have had their fill and all would have had a little water. As the pools cleared and filled, more could sip and wade and splash.

He held the cows back from a pool until it cleared a little, then got water for camp. The bread was pink that evening, and the coffee tasted muddy, but the water was more or less wet, and Millie and the baby enjoyed a scanty sponge bath before bed.

The next morning Joe said as he tied the packhorse's lead rope to the pack, "I'll go ahead to turn the cattle up the hill; you follow along and see the calves don't hang back and hide in the brush. Watch that buckskin one and the spotted one, they are tiredest and most apt to stop. Just work carefully around to the head of the canyon and start the herd down."

It was surprisingly easy to get the cows to go down the canyon, even the tired calves wanted to get out of the confined place. Sure enough, the buckskin calf tried to lag, but she ran at it and it scampered up to the herd. Except that she was stiff and sore, she felt better this morning, and by the time she turned to follow the cattle up the hill out of the canyon, her soreness had mostly worn away.

The hot spell that Joe dreaded caught up with them this day, but they were at a higher elevation and the cattle in better shape to stand it. In fact, it was pleasant along the ridge south of North Springs, not so dusty as the herd stepped out and dropped over into the head of Antelope Valley Now they were back in the loose sand again. It was like sugar for the animals to plod in, and a cloud of dust rose above the herd and settled impartially on her and the cattle in the choking heat.

She was determined to be more observant and noted that the wide valley really had no drainage; it was just a shallow swale filled with dunes of clean-looking blow sand. Interspersed with the dunes were clusters of sand bumps along the trail, and on the higher ridges lay knolls here and there with oak brush growing around the sides and over the tops. She wondered if each oak knoll was a sand hill covered by short brush, or a tall tree with the sand piled almost over it. This was a delicious fantasy, and she savored it.

The baby was more cooperative this morning, pointing and jabbering. In fact, the world looked much brighter.

They nooned at what they later named Whitbeck Knoll, and the cattle grazed the lush sandgrass and oak for an hour, then lay down to rest and chew their cuds. It was a long nooning, and when they started up the herd again, Joe cut back the spotted calf and its mother, since he didn't think the calf would make it the ten or twelve miles into the Roost Spring.

From the top of Whitbeck Knoll, Joe pointed out the landmarks to her. Across a low-lying stretch a similar knoll to that on which they were standing showed prominently. Joe said it was Deadman's Hill, and it lay beyond the Roost Spring.

"The black ridge top stretching east from the other end of Deadman is the dividing line to a different kind of country from this sand and the long gravel swales of the Roost Flats. Beyond it is the Twin Corrals, with Happy Canyon dropping off the south of it and the breaks and canyons of Horseshoe running north into the Green River.

"Beyond the Dirty Devil gorge, which is that low canyon, the Burr Desert rises to the Henry Mountains, which you can see in the distance. This is a big country, and a whole chunk of it is going to be mine—ours!" he finished exultantly. "Let's go get it."

Someone had to hold back the leaders so Joe put her out there while he brought up the drag. They still had the buckskin calf, but he was getting pretty tired, and if he didn't make it in, Joe planned to be around when he quit traveling. She was just to mosey along the trail in head of the cattle, not checking them too much, but not getting too far ahead, either. It wasn't dusty out there, and she felt a stab of self-pity for the miles she had slogged along in the dust with the drags.

When the cattle smelled water, she was not to try to hold them, she was to beat them to the trough and water her horse and she and Pearl were to get off down the canyon and keep the cows back from bunching near the slickrock dropoff where they could crowd one another off into the deep canyon below.

All went as he had predicted, and she and the baby had just gotten settled behind a rock when the first cows streamed around the small fenced patch on the steep sidehill and crowded up to the trough.

For the first time she actually looked at these cows her husband was willing to forego all the comforts of civilization for. They were a heterogenous bunch, no two the same color, sprung from the old Texas trailherds with here and there·one showing the larger size of some Durham or Shorthorn ancestor. Joe had said the whitefaced Herefords (he called them bald-faced) were the coming breed. There were a few of these in the herd; the rest were roan, both red and blue, or spotted in every color cows came in, with one solid black one. She counted six red ones, too. Durham color showed there, as well as in the red roans and the two white ones, although she did not judge them that closely.

Joe rode up finally and dropped the little yellow calf. A wicked looking old light red cow with needle-pointed horns rushed out to claim it. The little fellow had been the least of her worries for almost a hundred miles, Millie remembered, but now that someone had given him a much-needed lift, she was all concern. Millie mentioned this to Joe as he came up; he laughed and scratched his whiskered cheek.

"That's just cows," he remarked. "Pull one out of the mud and save its life and it will try to run you down and stomp you to death or hook your horse's guts out. Tail up a poor one in the spring and it will make a pass at you and like as not fall down again." He said all this with such affection that she looked at him critically.

Here was a real cowman who was doing what he really wanted to do. It might not turn out all right; she was still dubious about his dreams of developing water enough on this tumbled range; she could only try to imagine what other dangers of man and nature threatened them. But this husband of hers was where he wanted to be and he planned to conquer this vast waste and turn it into a home. And he trusted her to help.

To my mother a cow was a cow was a cow, and that settled the matter; to my father, each critter was an individual with needs and rights (under his direction) that he recognized and honored. He never quite believed that to his wife all cows looked alike, they had such personality to him. He didn't believe it, but he was forced to accept it.

"And tomorrow we rest," she said, "now that we are here."

"The hell we do," he told her. "If I can find that cow and spotted calf in time, we start out toward Horseshoe Canyon."

"What *for!*" She was dismayed. "I thought you wanted to come to the *Roost.*"

"I did, and here we are. But this whole country is called the Roost; we have come through the only open side, and this north open space stretches for only ten or twelve miles between the head of the Roost Canyon here and the breaks of Horseshoe on the east. But that is enough for these cows to turn right around and head back for the San Rafael to get stuck in the mud. By the time they water in the Roost Spring again, they are going to have lived here long enough to have forgotten the San Rafael River.

"Over that far ridge is another country just as big as this Roost Flats, and beyond it is the Spur that stretches north between Horseshoe and Millard, and back the other way from the Spur and over beyond Frenchy Seep, another high land of cedared ridges and open parks reaches to the dropoff into Under the Ledge. These canyons are deep, damn deep, and only a few rough trails lead off into them."

"You are going to run cattle on all *that?*"

"You bet, every inch of it, and it won't take me long to do it. A few years and I'll have an outfit here that all the smart alecs who advised me not to come will envy." He spoke prophetically; he lived to see it come true beyond his wildest dreams.

It was a big land, a good land, but it took a big man to tame it and to hold it against those who had not seen its possibilities. Only its isolation had kept it from being claimed before, but that didn't bother Joe Biddlecome a bit; and where he went—he took his family. Sure, things got tough sometimes, he would admit that; but not so tough as being separated from Millie and his children.

They camped back of the cattle and held them on the water all night. Joe nightherded them, riding the pack horse saving his saddlehorse. The next morning he put Millie on the trail out south to hold the cattle from leaving that way.

"Ern's got a few head running here; let them by if they want to come in or go back out, but make all ours go up the draw. I'll be back as soon as I locate that cow and spotted calf."

She sat and held her horse while Pearl picked up rocks and played in the dust of the trail. Some cows came down from the range above, and when she heard them coming she moved aside and let them go by.

After while these cows wanted back, but she had forgotten what they looked like and since she couldn't ask them if they belonged to Ern Wild, she threw rocks at them and yelled, making them go back up the wash with the others. Joe would have been really amazed at that. Aside from the fact that he knew his own cattle as personages, these were sleek and fat, not the dusty, high-flanked, rough-haired animals that had just made that long trip.

This was a sample of Millie's cow savvy; in the years to come she never learned or cared about cows. She just did what Joe told her and when the judgement was up to her, she swung wildly and missed as often as she hit. In the long run, Joe accepted it—he could hire a cowboy, but Millie was raising a family and he sure enjoyed them and her. If cowpunching was a side issue with her, he would just have to accept it, and he did.

My mother associated with rough men on the range all her life, and although she swore casually and liberally, she never competed with them on their own ground. This was partly due, of course, to time and customs. She violated tradition in riding astride and wearing pants, but she was well aware that she wasn't a man; she had no desire to be one and she made no effort to speak, look or act like one.

All this was far in the future. This June morning in 1909 Millie sat in the hot sun, under the meager shelter of one of Joe's castoff Stetsons, and turned the wrong cattle up the draw. Joe found his cow and calf, rested and wandering along in the tracks of the herd, and rode around behind them. In an hour or so he hustled them down the hill into the draw and over to the spring, where the cow supped with the few stragglers still hanging around the water.

Coming up out of the wash onto the bunch ground above the spring, he waved his wife in. With the high cutbanks from which to load her passenger, she soon joined him. He untied the pack horse from the corner post of the fence around the spring and turned him loose with the cattle. They started up the brushy draw, stirring out the few cattle shaded up in the catclaw bushes and shoved them along the trail. Presently the sides of the sandy wash dropped back and left a wide place; a stone chimney thrust up out of the bushes, where a cabin had been built and later burned.

Joe told her this was the lone habitation remnant on this whole range. This cabin had once housed Jack Cottrell and his wife, Ellen Tomlinson Cottrell and her family of three little Tomlinson boys, shortly after she and Jack were married.

"They say," Joe laughed, that Butch Cassidy and the Wild Bunch visited them often, and that these three little boys played the game of cops and robbers amongst the brush and rocks of this little valley with a new twist—it was always the U. S. Marshal that got shot!"

As they rode up the draw he complained of a sore throat, and Millie, scared, hoped that it was only a dryness from the dust. Several times she had seen him through attacks of quinsey, (a recurring abscess under the tonsil, which develops to a "head" eventually, and ruptures and drains) and he didn't need that again, and surely neither did she in this distant land. He felt pretty rotten by evening, and really sick the next morning. Her relief knew no bounds when her brother Offie overtook them, having followed the tracks of the herd.

"What happened to you?" Joe asked as they shook hands. He had always liked this big, handsome kid with his good-natured grin and snapping brown eyes. Offie had been raised on the farm on Utah Bottom; most of the range lore he knew had come from Joe, whom he idolized.

"Got to courtin'," he answered. "You're lucky I ever

made it at all." They rode over to Millie and Offie gave her a letter from her mother.

Joe rode on to point the cattle down along Blue John Canyon, which they were approaching, and Offie fell in beside her.

"I'm so glad you're here," she said. "Joe thinks he has quinsey."

"Noticed he talked funny," her brother answered. "But what the hell are you and Pearl doing here? Let me take her for a while."

It was good to flex her tired arms and shoulders. But she pondered briefly how to answer him.

"I just am," she said. "I guess I'm going to be here from now on. I have followed as best I could ever since we were married."

"But *horseback*—with a kid! That's a little rough, isn't it?"

"More than a little this trip, but things will be better now we are here," she spoke hopefully.

Her brother gave her a long, frowning look, then turned aside to haze a cow up with the bunch. Pearl was delighted, this was fun "Go Horsey," with some action to it.

They dropped the herd over the Sandslide into Horseshoe Canyon that night and the next day hazed them up the canyon and out into what they later called the Lower Pasture. Joe was really sick now, exhausted by his night and day trek as well as all those months of worry and indecision. My mother remembers this as the worst attack of quinsey he ever suffered—in fact that she ever saw. By morning he was in great pain, could no longer swallow water and was feverish and irritable.

They were camped under a tree on a little sandbar of the canyon near a rock water tank, and Millie sponged his face and chest from time to time. They had no medicine of any kind, but mighty few drugs would have helped him at that stage.

When morning finally dawned, Offie brought in his horse and mule and announced he was going home. "The cows are set, the horses have got enough feed for a few days here in the canyon, and I'm getting behind in my courtin'."

"But, Offie," she felt the world fall away beneath her feet. "You can't leave us like this. Joe is a mighty sick man."

"He sure is, for a fact." Offie hesitated, thinking, then brightened. "But he never has died with quinsey."

"He never has been this bad before."

"Cheer up, Sis, things will be fine," and he started to throw his pack on the mule.

"But, Offie, when are you coming back?"

"I ain't." He ducked under the mule's neck and looked at her in puzzlement. "I just come in the first place because Joe sent for me to drive the wagon out and bring you and the baby. Sorry I was too late to do that, but I've got things to do, too."

Joe stirred and she went to him. She dropped down beside him and begged him to ask Offie to stay another day, which should see him through. This big man was never subservient at best, and he was not at his best this morning.

"Let him go," he croaked. "If he can't see how bad we need him, the hell with him. I'm not going to get down on my knees to him for anything. I'll be all right."

She rose and went back to Offie; she could beg and she did.

"I don't see what's got you so upset. Even if Joe died (and he won't) you and Pearl could ride right back the way you came—in half the time without cattle to drive."

"How? How would I know which way to go?"

"Just follow the cow tracks back. God, Millie, it's as plain as a wagon road."

How could she tell him that to her it was the most wonderful thing in the world that men could look at tracks and tell which way the animal had been going. How could she make him understand that at any point along that back trail she could get mixed up and come right back here, never knowing the difference for miles and miles out on the desert.

"Joe is OK, you'll see. Well, *adios,* come over and see us some time. I'll tell Mama you got here." He mounted and rode whistling down the canyon.

The day dragged on. If that's the way it is going to be, that's the way it is going to be, she thought. As Joe's condition worsened toward night, she made her decision. She'd never, never saddle a horse if he died. She'd rather die here of starvation than out on that awful desert alone.

That night the throat abscess broke. She was sitting beside him, holding his hand, and had dropped off to sleep. Suddenly he leaped up coughing and spitting. Stepping clear of the camp, he retched and coughed for a few minutes.

Such a flood of relief washed over Millie as she was ever to know. He would be all right; he had come through another attack of quinsey, the worst she had ever seen. All he needed now was sleep, and in a few hours he would waken as hungry as a dog. She would then pound up some jerky (dried beef) into shreds, boil it in the frying pan and thicken it with some flour. Sowbelly and pone (salt pork and dutch oven bread) were a little coarse for his raw throat for a day or two.

They were out of the woods now. When he was stronger Joe would start looking over his range and making plans to conquer the Roost for his own. Perhaps it was the place to build his kingdom as he said, but there had been times in the past 24 hours when she had looked upon Robbers Roost as the place where they would all meet their Maker.

The original Roost Spring troughs being placed by my father and Uncle Offie.

3

Settling In

As soon as Joe had explored his domain a little closer, and had gained his strength back, they returned to San Rafael for the wagon and the rest of their belongings. The trip back was pleasant; Joe carried the baby and they rode right along. The cabin on the bank of the river (washed out by floods a few years later) looked good to her, but smaller some way.

The next day while she packed, Joe went up and bought the saddle from Gillies, and checked for cows. He asked if any of the boys at the ranch had seen any cows he had missed, and they told him they hadn't found even one. They were impressed—a man *had* to miss a few!

Again, Gillies tried to dissuade him, and again my father swore stubbornly he was going to build a cattle empire at the Roost. As they shook hands at parting, Gillies wished him luck with more hope than faith.

The pack horse and extra saddle horse had had a couple of day's rest, and when hitched to the wagon, pulled out steadily up Dugout Wash in the early morning. The wagon held all they owned, but it was not overloaded. The heaviest

thing by far was the barrel of water for the horses that night at
the Gap in Black Ridge. It wouldn't be enough, portioned out
to the team, the two he was leading and the one that followed,
but it would keep them from straying off that night looking
for water. It was all he could lug up the steep, sandy slope.
The open-topped barrel was covered with a piece of tarp and
and extra barrel hoop pounded down over the tarp to make a
snug slop-proof cover.

It was late in June, and summer had set in for sure. The
desert sands reflected the glare of the sun as they crawled
slowly across the wastes of North Springs wash the next day.
The wagon heaved over sand bumps, first on one side then
the other. Finally they dropped over into the level gravel wash
bottom and made good time from there into North Springs.

Joe watered the horses and took them out on the flats
above the canyon to graze while Millie cooked supper on the
campfire and made the bed in the wagon. The baby played
around and walked unsteadily up and down the damp banks
of the wash, enjoying the cool wetness after the searing dehy-
dration of the day.

The next forenoon when they dropped over into Antelope
Valley, they didn't go up the sand-bump choked draw, but
crossed and followed an easy swale toward the cedars on the
far ridge. There was an ancient road here, nearly obliterated,
which had been used by Blue John when he drove a wagon-
load of supplies out for the Wild Bunch. Soon they came to
scattered cedars and dropped over into the converging sand-
draws of a canyon. To their left was an upheaval of canyon
and butte and ledge.

"Horseshoe Canyon," Joe pointed.

"Where our cattle are?"

"That's right. Look familiar?"

"Nothing in this whole country looks familiar to me.
I think we have driven off the edge of the world."

"I'd think so, too," he laughed, "if there wasn't such a helluva lot of world all around us."

Pulling through heavy sand patches and rattling over slick rock, they crossed the breaks of the canyon head, climbed a short ridge and broke out onto the northeastern edge of Roost Flats, and my mother was thrilled to recognize where she was. They had taken the cattle near here to cross that broken country into Horseshoe. Soon after topping out, they crossed the ribbon of roughened earth that she recognized as the tracks of the herd they had driven.

"We are away off from the Roost Spring, aren't we?" she worried.

"Yes, there is a spring along the ridge here, over in the Horseshoe breaks and we'll camp there. Let's call it Blue John."

This was the first name they gave to the country. Robbers Roost was a designation for all of it, and had been applied too far back to remember. A few other names had been used for some of the more prominent features—French Seep, Twin Corrals, The Spur, and Millard Canyon. They learned later that they had misunderstood this name; instead of honoring a president, it was named for an undistinguished "Miller" who did nothing more than leave this small, mistaken mark on the map. Later, they also misunderstood the name of the Gordons, which they heard from the French sheepmen who were taking their herds through the Roost to Under the Ledge for wintering. These sheepmen had called the flats between French Seep and Land's End "The French Gardens" because of their lush beauty.

Presently they dropped off the ridge into a deep wash and after negotiating some scarey sidehills in the bright red badlands, my father pulled up to a ledge and said, "This is it."

Millie hated Blue John on sight. It was down over the ridge from the Roost Flats; she couldn't see half a mile.

If they built their ranch out where the flats swept up toward Deadman's Hill where she could see around, it was half a mile from water. If they built here, as her husband had planned, she could see a red rock wall on one side, and scattered cedars and sun-blasted sharp little hills on the other three sides. There was no view in any direction; in all this beautiful land she was to be buried in an ugly, sere gully.

In July of that first year, they left the wagon and most of their stuff at Blue John and moved camp by packhorse to the Spur, where Joe watched his herd settle into a new country. As the nights grew chillier in September, he knew he had to find a place for his family for the winter, especially as they were expecting in February.

The closest town to the Roost was Hanksville, about 45 horseback miles west. If they established their home there he could come in every few weeks. If they settled in Green River, which was some 75 miles north, he couldn't possibly make the trip more than once or twice during the cold weather. He planned to spend his winter right out with the cattle, moving them to sheltered spots, and bringing them through this first bad season practically one by one.

It was a tough choice to make, but finally they opted for Hanksville and rode over. They found a small, two-room cabin with a sod roof and moved in. He bought the place in a year or two and put up a well-built log cabin, two rooms and a high loft that made another room upstairs for a bedroom. This was a good house, so well built, in fact, that it was cheaper to burn it in the 1960s when the land was cleared for a highway, than to tear it down. It had a shingle roof which had lasted for over fifty years.

Millie had lived near Mormons all her life, but not really among them. Moab was settled by this group, but the Scharfs had very little contact with them; most of their business and social connections were at Cisco, where the railroad people dominated. Actually her first experience among the Mormons was when I was born in Ferron in 1907.

Joe had grown up in a Mormon family. His mother was a devout adherent, converted in her native Wales, making her way to Utah in her late teens. She had married John Reid, and after his death she married George Biddlecome. They had pioneered in the Castle Valley area, near Ferron. After he was drowned in Ferron Creek in 1901, she continued her duties as midwife, working with doctors when possible, but mostly alone. Most of the babies of Emery County around the turn of the century had their first breath spanked into them by Grandma Biddlecome, as she was familiarly called.

Her household was strictly Mormon; in fact, the family had been so religious during his growing up that my father had pulled out when he was about 12 and gone to live with the Swasey family, who were considerably more broadminded, although they were themselves a polygamous family. My father was bitterly anti-Mormon all his life, although he respected his mother's belief, even giving her money to do Temple Work when she came to live with us after I was partly grown.

Since Millie's conviction that Mormons were more superstitious than religious never changed to any degree, their choice of Hanksville was unfortunate. This small town had been re-named from Gray's Valley when Ebeneezer Hanks took one of his plural wives and four of his married daughters and their families there during the Manifesto days of polygamy, around 1890. Their progeny still lived there when the Biddlecomes moved in.

The McDougalls were the leading family. Mrs. McDougall was the postmistress, which shed considerable luster on the family. Most of their children were married and settled around them, but their youngest daughter, Jessie, was still home and acclaimed the village belle. The Biddlecomes were not the only non-Mormons, the Webers were Gentiles also: Gentiles being anyone of a different religious persuasion. Celia Weber was one of Millie's closest friends, but several of the Latter-day Saint women were good neighbors, too. Mrs. Rufe Stoddard was one of these, and Alice Hanks and Millie were close friends all their lives. In fact, she was doing all right that first winter when her brother Offie came to visit and the situation fell apart.

Offie immediately fell in love with Jessie McDougall and that did it! Millie raised the roof—she also raised hell, and she made herself a burgeoning crop of enemies of a powerful and somewhat ruthless tribe. As the years went by, she learned to accept Jessie and the McDougalls laid off after a while, but she was never a part of the town socially, and was never happy there. She spent the next summer and winter in Hanksville, but took her small girls (Pearl was three and Hazel a year past in February) to the Roost for the next summer. She spent only the coldest months in town the next few years, moving to the cattle range as soon as the promise of spring released her.

That first fall, after he had his family settled, Joe worked like a dog placing his cattle for winter. In those days, snow fell deeper, and he scattered his cows by twos and threes into sheltered canyons and places where they could forage for a month or so during the coldest months. He had heard stories of how high the snow got here—"Ten Utes deep!"—and he put a few cows in a gully here and a few along a cedared sidehill over there. Feed was no item, grass and browse were lush everywhere as long as they were not covered with three feet of snow.

One day in late October he rode up on a ridge to see a vast cloud of dust coming up the swale in the head of Roost Flats. The breeze brought the tinkle of sheep bells as well as the wooly smell. He rode down and greeted the herder, Karl Seely, whom he'd grown up with. There was no reason for any but the most cordial relations; sheep could not winter at the Roost but were taken Under the Ledge, and that was where Karl was headed. He said Noe Aubert and Big Henry Dusserre were right behind him with their herd, probably going into Happy Canyon as they usually did.

Joe knew Noe Aubert, he had met him at the French ranch just below the Gillies ranch on the San Rafael, but he had never met Big Henry (Honore) Dusserre.

When the Frenchmen's herd came along, Joe rode up to it. Big Henry had heard about this fool who had taken his cows to the Roost to lose them, but as he watched this tall, handsome fellow ride toward him, he didn't think he'd lose. Joe saw a powerful man, getting a bit grizzled in the temples, wide-faced and bullet-headed, with sharp grey eyes almost hidden in squint wrinkles from living outdoors all his life.

They got off their horses to rest and talk, each recognizing what a magnificent man the other was. That morning of winey October air with its smell of sheep, smell of horses and dust, Henry Dusserre, with his dogs crouched at his feet, and Joe Biddlecome, holding his reins loosely, forged a friendship that spanned their lifetimes and that of their children.

The third winter Millie spent in Hanksville she had a baby born dead, or that died soon afterward. She still had Pearl, four and Hazel, two, and the next summer she announced she had had it "clear up to here" in Hanksville. She pointed out that as she remembered the deal, she was to spend the summers at the Roost. Offie and Jessie were married about this time, and feeling was running pretty high.

Hazel was still too small to hang on, but I was old enough to ride on a pillow tied behind the cantle of the saddle. I hung onto the rider, learning that a loose hold was better than hanging tightly, and while I could balance myself to some degree with my legs, they were still too short to reach to a horse's ticklish flanks, so things went well.

That summer and the next, when our parents did all their

own riding, Papa carried Hazel mostly, but often handed her to her mother while he went flying off after a cow or a bunch of them. When he needed her help, Mama would park us kids in or under a tree. It was all right as long as the old folks were in sight, but I remember that there was a sinking feeling to be set off in a tree and left with nothing but puffs of dust to show which direction they had taken. And these fears would have been well-founded, too, if we had had to depend on our mother to locate us again; but Joe Biddlecome had such an uncanny inbuilt orientation, sense of direction, and oneness with his surroundings that he never missed a target an inch, day or night.

The summer I was seven and Hazel, five, was the last year we "rode behind." That winter Papa traded somewhere for a small white pony we called Yanaho and the next spring we transferred to him. We didn't have stirrups, though, until I was nine, when we each got a horse. Mine was Darkey and Hazel had Tom Mule.

4

Cow Camp Etiquette and Customs

ALTHOUGH WE LIVED IN COW camps with the simplest of conveniences and equipment, never think we did not have a strict code of deportment and etiquette. Since the casual visitor usually understood the system, it must have been prevalent over the West in that early day. Remember these men were tough characters, many of them outside the law, and all of them living a life that separated the men from the boys early. Their work was grinding; horseback riding day by day is the hardest work in the world. Their comforts were mostly lacking and keeping a minimal standard of cleanliness was a tough project.

The horseman's profession was a fast-paced one and fraught with crises, large and small. Therefore, these men developed a vocabulary of considerable color. We swore casually and continually (my mother still does at the age of 91), but there were strict taboos in this, too. No dirty words were used, at least in mixed company, and no one swore at another person. When Owen Wister's Virginian told Trampas, who had called him a , "When you say that, *smile*" we knew exactly what he meant. And we interpreted the blank as sonofabitch rather than any obscene expression.

Make no mistake about it, the men we associated with were tough enough to survive in the hardest situation in human experience outside of downright war, but while I was growing up I never heard an offcolor joke or a dirty word from any of them; my mother and sister and I were treated with consideration and respect. We were always ladies, too, within the framework of existing conditions, of course. We worked cattle as efficiently as men, rode as expertly, slept in beds on the ground, ate from the frying pan and sought a concealing cedar for privacy exactly as did the cowboys visiting or working for us.

When we girls were small we couldn't take the day-to-day cowpunching all the time, and when she could, Mama stayed in camp with us and rested for an afternoon or even for all day. For cowboys, camp was mainly for eating and sleeping, but what little social life they did have was centered there, so most of the finer points of etiquette concerned camp life. Although which fork to use was no problem, there being no forks, there were rules.

When every ounce of equipment is carried on the back of a mule, there isn't much excess baggage. The usual camp utensils consisted of a frying pan, coffee pot, dutch oven and a cup apiece for the crew. If we needed a spoon, Papa whittled one out of a clean stick. The staples of coffee, salt, sugar, etc., were carried in small canvas bags, tied with a string, the color of the string indicating the contents of the sack as we became accustomed to using them. The color of the sacks started out canvas white, but gradually picked up dinginess from the pack bags, the campfire utensils and the red sand that covered and colored everything. A slovenly camp that was thrown into packbags all together and that was dirty and meager was referred to as "a greasy sack outfit," but ours was never that.

When it was time to cook a meal, one of our parents, usually my mother, chunked the flour sack down solidly to give it a good, flat bottom, pressed the top down firmly, then untied it and rolled down the edge of the sack and pressed the flour out to make a hole in the center. Into this hole she stirred a little baking powder (we preferred Schillings, it was never bitter) and salt, scraping loose some of the flour to mix with these ingredients. Then she poured in a couple of cups of water and with a stick whittled clean, and often carried in the flour sack, she stirred a dough stiff enough to handle.

In the meantime the dutch oven and lid had been heating on the fire. Using a long stick for a poker, the dutch oven was hauled in, swabbed clean, often with a piece of gunny sack, and a dollop of dough dropped in and pressed out into a pone. If there was grease available, some was used, or often a piece of bacon was rubbed over the hot oven, but usually the pone was cooked in the floured, hot oven without sticking. Teflon— hah! A few coals were raked aside from the fire, the dutch oven set on them and the lid, laden with coals, added.

Getting these coals up over the high rim of the lid was a pretty good trick. With the poker she shoved the lid into the fire, pushing up a bank of coals. When she had enough raked onto the lid, she lifted it again and (this was important!) tapped it hard enough against the dutch oven to shake loose the sand clinging to the bottom of the lid, but not hard enough to spill sand and coals from the top into the dutch oven. If she didn't bring this off, she said dammit and set the lid on anyway. In this waste of clean, red sand, what was a little more or less in the food? The saying was, "Never mind, we all eat *over* a ton of sand every day, anyway."

We usually had beef, even when our cattle were few and this was a sacrifice. My father felt that beef, bread, coffee, with a little jam for dessert was all any normal human being needed for a balanced diet. Mama, raised on the Utah Bottom farm where she had been accustomed to all kinds of vegetables and fruit, found this menu pretty grim. Even potatoes were too heavy to carry.

Many years later, on their way to town with the steers, Papa asked her what she was going to do first when she got to town—they had been talking about her going home for a visit with her folks. She rode along for a bit, then brought her vision back from the Utah Bottom and turned her big brown eyes up to him and said: "I'm going to eat some 'taters and ice cream." This was a family joke for years; it was about as high as a person could live.

In the summer time a beef (usually a calf) was killed in the evening, and allowed to cool out in the dry, bracing air of this high country night. The next morning before sunup it was sacked and rolled into a bedroll, which retained the cool temperature until evening, when the meat was hung to air again. Meat will keep a week or ten days in the hottest weather on the desert if the pack is not broken by opening the bedroll during the day.

If we didn't have beef, we used bacon or sowbelly (salt pork), but it was a poor substitute; so it was necessary to preserve the beef as best we could. In later years we bottled meat with a pressure cooker, but in the early days at the Roost we either cured or jerked it.

We cured it by cutting the bone out of a hind quarter of a calf and salting it liberally, adding pepper and sometimes spices to discourage the blowflies. This was done in the evening, the meat rolled and sacked to drain all night then treated as fresh meat.

There are almost as many recipes for making jerky as there are people making it, but basically it is meat cut into strips, salted and hung to dry. In hot weather, it is usually hung on some kind of rack with a smoky fire under it to keep off the flies. Cured meat was sliced and fried like fresh meat, but usually jerky was pounded up and a gravy made over it.

After jerky was carried for a while, it developed beetles and hairy crawling things that Mama and we girls considered vermin, and we wouldn't eat it. Even today I view stories of the nutritious pemmican that the trappers and explorers carried for emergency food with more than a grain of suspicion.

Killing a beef was a time for real rejoicing; bacon is a poor substitute for steak. In the summer time a three or four-month-old calf carcass could be kept fresh until it was eaten, and the meat was simply superb.

My father did the butchering, helped, no doubt, by the hired man, but with much admonishment against scoring the hide, if he planned to use it in a project. This made it almost impossible for anyone but him to do the actual skinning. Calf hides were not usually used, however, they were too tender to make good strings.

The animal, after being shot and bled thoroughly, was strung up in a tree by a gambrel stick between the hind legs, and pulled to a high limb by a lasso rope. After the skin was removed, the entrails were let down, and there was a flurry of interest as to whether or not the marrowguts were good. If the calf had been old enough to eat grass, they were not, since we were all well aware that the marrowguts were the small intestine and a part of the digestive system of the calf. However, if the calf was eating only milk, the marrowguts, when cut open, revealed a pink, solid looking interior, and they were "good." Papa then cut loose a couple of feet or a yard or so for the first meal.

We didn't like liver, and we seldom used it; I still think sweetbread is inedible. However, the heart was looked on with approval, and it too, was saved for the first meal.

For supper after killing a beef, we had marrowguts, heart, and finished out with ribs, cut in sections and cooked to a crisp brown in the frying pan or dutch oven. The marrowguts were cut into pieces about an inch or two long and as they fried, they curled until they were almost little circles, and they were simply delicious.

There was another gourmet item that we never ate when I was a kid, but which is acclaimed by range folk; that is "mountain oysters." We called them—well, shucks! we called them calf nuts. They were a byproduct of branding, when the male calves were castrated and the nuts either tossed into the corral dust to be nosed out by the dog, or laid out on a log to be taken home for supper. My mother viewed them with disfavor, thinking it was somehow savage to eat part of an animal that was up roaming around.

When removed from the calf, the oysters are about the size of a small sausage in the younger animals up to about the size of half a weiner in the larger calves. And they have a cord about four or five inches long attached to one end. Although spoken of as pairs, they are not in pairs actually, just in twos, so to speak.

These were cleaned by splitting the tough, outside covering and scooping out the pink, delicate gland with the thumb. Tossed into salted water, until a couple of dozen were cleaned, they were drained, rolled in flour and fried.

Another way calf nuts were cooked was *au naturel* in the branding fire. After the day's work was done, we turned the cattle out of the corral, then stood around and rested for a few minutes before burying the branding fire, gathering up the paraphernalia and going to camp. In later years after I had married and had a family, my boys—Joe, Jack and later Noel—would take the calf nuts they had salvaged and lay them in the coals of the branding fire. When these popped open and the inside browned, the boys thought they were fine eating. I inherited my mother's squeamishness, but I was always assured I was missing a treat!

In a pack outfit, everything gets squashed, and in hot

weather a can of grease was simply out of the question. Our only supply was tallow, which could be carried like fresh meat. After the fresh meat was gone, a little bacon held all the grease we required. This tallow was cut into bits into the frying pan and the steak laid on top of it to cook. There was just enough grease when the meat was cooked to go with the jam, poured into the frying pan, to make the pieces of pone dipped into it most delicious.

When the coffee boiled it was settled with a half cup or so of cold water, the pot pulled to a few coals to keep hot, and the meal was ready. The frying pan was set in the middle of a piece of tarp and everyone gathered round. It was bad manners to crowd in too close.

We all carried pocket knives and everyone had his open for business. The one nearest the bread sack took out a pone and held it toward his neighbor, who took hold of it. Number one then cut off about a third or a fourth of the pone, the neighbor held it out to the diner next to him, and, holding it, one of them cut it in two. These pieces of pone were then split and a piece of meat put between, or more commonly, the meat was put on top of the bread with a small piece of crust on top to put the thumb on, both because the meat was greasy and because it was hot. Bite-sized pieces were then cut from the meat, speared on the point of the knife blade and carried to the mouth.

Sometimes there was corn or pork-and-beans or gravy. In that case, the meat was pushed to one side and the addition was warmed up or cooked in the same pan. To eat this, a small crust was broken from the bread and carefully dipped into the food, scooping up a reasonable bite. It wasn't good manners to put this bitten-off-from bread back into the food everyone was eating; you used a fresh bread crust each time, and you carefully kept from putting your fingers into the food, too. Jam was eaten the same way.

Water was always scarce. Canteens were not used until I was pretty well grown, and at first all the water we used was carried in water bags. They were such a nuisance that we preferred to go all day without a drink rather than have them flapping and flopping around, always in the way. Usually they were taken in when the loose horses were taken to water and brought back sometimes for miles to camp.

To wash our hands, someone poured a little water on the washer's hands and the soap. A lather was worked up then rinsed off. If water was *really* scarce, this took less than half a cupful, but could be a luxurious rite with a whole cupful. Often several of us washed at the same time, and had fun doing it.

The frying pan was cleaned by heating a cup or so of water in it and scrubbing it vigorously with a scrubber made of grass or brush folded double to make a heavy, effective scratcher. The cups were never washed, except with a table-spoonful or so of coffee before use. Each man had his own, and took care of it himself, although they were carried in the pack.

Beds were of quilts, mostly woolen, with heavy, soft woolen blankets to sleep between; my father's bedding was made specially long by Mama to cover his extra length. There was one universal item of bedding and that was the bedtarp. It was a light, tightly woven white canvas about 8' x 14' or 8' x 16', with snaps and rings on the sides. Theoretically these snapped together to make a bed roll, but we must have folded ours differently because these rings and snaps were just a nuisance. In this tarp the bed was rolled tightly every morning to keep it clean. I was hopeful, too, that mine was rolled too tightly for scorpions and other desert denizens to crawl into it.

We didn't use tents except in the winter time or in semi-permanent camps. During a rainy night, the tarp, being rela-tively waterproof, could be ballooned up over our heads to keep the drops from spattering in our faces. In a hard rain, however, it didn't really keep us dry, because wet canvas with the inside seal broken by rubbing, leaks like cheesecloth. Pools might collect on the top of the bed, too, and the unwary sleeper often turned over and funnelled these directly into the warm bed beneath.

In the summer a bed would dry in a couple of hours of hot sun the next morning, or if not, we toughed it out until a sunny day did provide a dry bed. We didn't ride much during rainy weather, because the cattle scattered and sought shelter so that they were hard to find, and my father usually spent a day or so in camp repairing saddles and equipment. Drying the bedding was no problem.

All of the Roost is a red sand country, and the places where a camp can be made on relatively level slickrock are rare. Therefore, everyone moved around camp very carefully. When Mama started to ride, she had broken with tradition enough to ride astride, so the first few years she wore riding skirts. These were a real inconvenience; when she sat down, we little girls kicked sand on them, and when she stood up this sand billowed out onto everything. Finally, she just wore bib overalls. We girls wore bib overalls when we were small, but Levis when we grew up—more of that later.

There was usually a light breeze, so that one never rode up to camp preceded by his dust; or ever walked around on the upwind side of the cooking area. Saddles were taken off and piled a bit out of camp, both to be out of the way and to be safe from damage.

We were taught to pile our saddle on its side, with the skirts and fenders straight, and lay the blankets over it, both to protect it from the sun if we didn't ride the next day and to dry the blankets. We kept our blankets clean, using only Navajos next to our horses, and we never had a sore-backed horse. We considered it gauche and mighty poor form to pull a saddle off and drop it flat as some did, and our saddles showed the care we took of them.

We used water from springs, clear and sweet, if we could get it, but sometimes we had to use flood water out of the rock tanks, and it was always red. Clay from the dark lenses of Carmel and other red beds, washed down and never wholly settled out of the water. Always the bread was pinkish, and all clothing took on the rich hue of this red country. Mama often had to wash clothes for us in this water, so she made our underwear of black sateen. My grandmother thought this was terrible, but these garments after washing felt fresh, and they smelled clean and with that, she had to be content.

Houseflies were never a problem in camp, there just weren't any. Big green bottle flies which we called blow flies, came around a little and the meat had to be protected from them, but they didn't bother anything else.

Of course, there wasn't enough water to breed mosquitoes, but the camp on Hans Flat one summer suffered a plague of yellow jackets. None of the family was especially allergic to the stings, although Hazel did react a bit to them, and both of us little girls sent up stabbed shrieks several times a day. We just rubbed the throbbing sting for a few seconds; there was nothing to treat it with, so we didn't.

These flying bullets were voracious. One would settle on a piece of meat, take a good hold with his legs and cut around quickly with his sharp pincers, flying off in two or three seconds with a chunk about the size of a pea. The yellow jacket nests were in stumps and roots of trees or catclaw bushes, and the swarms frantically stored food in them to carry the colony over the winter. Seemingly almost anything they could get and carry was stored.

Mama told us that one time on San Rafael someone had caught a big carp fish. It wasn't edible, but for some reason, Papa hung it up in a tree. Yellow jackets were bad that season, too, and she said they completely cleaned and polished the entire skeleton of that carp—there wasn't a shred of meat left on it anywhere.

When I was growing up, our whole life centered around horses; they were our whole working life and most of our recreation centered around them some way. Casual conversation was 90% horse, and everybody traded horses all the time.

Although Butch Cassidy and the Wild Bunch didn't come back to the Roost after we went there, riders did stray through from time to time. They were welcome, indeed, bringing companionship and often a few days' or a winter's help, and they always had a string of horses, which they traded as they traveled. One fellow brought in quite a cavvy one fall, and in the spring when he got ready to move on, both he and my father were a little hazy as to where their trading had left off; they had done so much of it on such limited numbers for several months that it was hard to keep track of.

While my mother took no part in this horse conversation, not being a gabby woman anyway, this was not the case with us little girls. We often complicated a horse trade.

One time we had on hand a little roan horse that was corral balky, he didn't want to leave the corral and camp. Since we small riders were not strong enough to jerk him around, we would have to go round and round the corral until someone came back and rescued us by leading him off a few hundred yards. This was hard on the ego.

We also owned Babe, a big roan horse, one of those nondescript, unimpressive horses, not too smart, that do the bulk of the hard work but are lost as a rope horse or in other exacting work. Every string had one or two. Why Papa was willing to trade Babe is a mystery; the other fellow must have had a pretty choice item.

We little girls looked the other horse over critically and when our father asked us, partly in fun and partly to show us off, what we thought, I, remembering that I had been rescued just the day before from a circle around and around the corral, said, "Looks better than that roan, corral-balky sonofabitch." We tried to point out the other roan to the fellow, but there was no trade and we never regretted it.

This was about the time we got Button. Papa had been riding on the San Rafael desert and stopped to camp with someone who had this little bay horse with white hind stockings. Button was most attractive, he had sort of a black mottling when he was fat and sleek, and he had a beautiful head with large, intelligent eyes. His mane was long and silky, and I especially remember his graceful, sweeping tail.

Papa opined the horse would make a good mount for "Tootsie" who wanted something gentle. The owner assured him by saying, "Try him." So my father did. He tossed on his saddle, cinched it down and without stepping the horse up to get him used to the situation, stepped aboard.

Button bucked across the camp, and Papa was hard pressed to stay with him. He liked the horse, anyway, and went ahead and acquired him. We owned Button until he died of old age some twenty years later, and he never bucked again.

Bucked, no; ran away, yes—many times. My mother was no horseman and made no pretense in that direction. There was only one way to get from here to over there, and that was on a horse, so she did, but it was a means to an end, and she neither liked nor disliked her mount—for all the feeling she had for her horse, she might have been riding a bicycle. That is, until she got Red Fox, but that is another story.

Cattle on the open range grow wild and run away, especially in the cedars, as soon as they see, hear or smell a man. We were taught to hold them up, always, until they quieted, and our cattle, with notable exceptions were not supposed to be wild—just frisky.

Mama would start out to hold them up with good intentions but bad judgement, because she usually waited too long. Giving Button the rein and a jab with the spurs, she was off, clinging and riding desperately, because Button could and did run, dodging trees and crashing through brush and up or down rocky hillsides. She would try to keep control of the situation, but any sawing on the reins or slapping with the romal or spurring just made him angry. He knew what he was supposed to do, get ahead of the cattle, and he ran until he did or lost them in the thick trees.

Then he and Mama would back trail, cattle forgotten, Mama keeping a sharp lookout for her hair "rats" (women rolled their hair over wads of hair to make the coiffure fancier) and other scattered equipment. This went on for years, until one day she got back to camp a little early, and instead of combing her hair neatly around the rats again, she grabbed the embroidery scissors from her fancy-work bag and cut it off more or less straight around.

In those days only shady ladies had bobbed hair, and while Papa thought it was a hilarious way to solve her problem (Button never ran away with anyone else, and I don't think Papa ever really believed he did with Mama), he foresaw snide remarks. Going along with the joke and her request, he sat her down on the wagon tongue and cut her hair short like a man's. This was most becoming to her little round face, and all summer whenever he looked at her, he would be overcome with affection and instead of hugging her, he rubbed her hair with his knuckles. By fall her hair was luxurious and long enough to comb around rats again, but thinly.

My mother on Browney.

5

The Killing of Shoot-'Em-Up-Bill

DURING THE LAST summer that little Hazel and I rode behind our parents on their saddlehorses, the Biddlecomes went visiting. Above the Gillies ranch on the San Rafael, where the Green-River-Hanksville road crossed, lay the oldest ranch on the river. It had been settled by the Halverson brothers, Henry and Chris, but now was owned by Bill Tomlinson, one of the little boys who had played cops-and-robbers around the cabin above Roost Spring. He had married Martha Warner, who had been raised at Woodside.

Martha and her brother Jim, after their father's death, were sent to St. Ann's orphanage in Salt Lake City where she received a fine education, including music. She played the piano well, in spite of a crippled arm, and the Tomlinsons owned a piano, which impressed Hazel and me very much. Music had played a minor part in our lives up to this point, with harmonicas (we called them mouth-harps) being about the only instrument with which we were familiar. During the winter time in Hanksville, sometimes we went with our parents up to Grandma and Grandpa Ekkers' place and listened to their phonograph, an Edison that played cylinder records. But a piano!—

I don't know how we became friendly with the Tomlinsons, but it seems to have been of some standing by 1915,
the first time I can remember going there. We got a late start,
or we skipped camping at North Springs; anyway, we hit
San Rafael at Dugout on the Harris Bottoms long after dark.
I remember it well, because as we were planning to camp
we stirred up a rattlesnake, but it was jet dark and we had to
let him go. But we rode on some farther to make camp.

Rattlesnakes were rather common, and horned toads were
everywhere when I was a child. Now you seldom see the
former and it has been years and years since anyone has
reported the latter. We killed the rattlesnakes, which were the
small desert variety, but we loved the horned toads, and trans-
ported them whenever feasible to a red ant hill where they sat
licking up the ants until they were stuffed.

I remember that although it was too dark to see as we
rode out on the river bottom that night, there were other senses
to let us know where we were. We could hear the lapping
and gurgling of the river currents; taste the bitter alkali in
the dust; and smell the wetness of the night air after the sere
day, even flavored as it was by the acridness of the blue mud of
the river banks. The saltgrass of the flat had a special odor,
and the cottonwoods were spicily aromatic. There is a wonderful lift to the scent of cottonwoods—they grow only where there
is water close to the surface, and their aroma defines life to us
desert folk as we seek their hospitable shelter.

Making camp near the river we gathered a little wood
and cooked a meager supper and spread our beds. I was a bit
nervous about that rattlesnake, having heard stories of a man's
awakening with a snake coiled on his chest, both of them afraid
to move, and other such folk tales; but this night we were all
too tired to care much.

We rode up the river the next day and came into the
Tomlinson ranch in the afternoon. It was wonderful, we

admired Martha's household, and the two little girls just younger than we were (Wilda between Hazel and me and Muriel just a few months younger than Hazel) were fine playmates.

During the evening we heard the grownups talk as we played on the floor in a corner of the room, but if subsequent events the next day hadn't set it in mind, I probably would never have recalled it. Bill was telling my father about the problems they were having with Shoot-'Em-Up-Bill Hatfield, one of the Kentucky Hatfields, who had set up camp in a dugout against the ledge across the river.

The Pressett family, Tomlinson's mother and stepfather and their little daughter just our age, and Mel and Ed Cottrell from her former marriage, lived at the southern end of the cable bridge spanning the river, and farmed a part of Bill's fields. Bill's brother, Mirt, and his family had lived across the road from the Pressetts, but they had moved away, leaving the old folks somewhat isolated. Shoot-'Em-Up was in the habit of coming over drunk and riding into their yard shouting threats and cursing them.

Before coming to this part of the country a few years before, Shoot-'Em-Up had had a narrow brush with the law. In Cameo, Colorado, he and a fellow were having a fight and the fellow's girl ran between them. Shoot-'Em-Up made a swipe at the fellow with a heavy poker and hit the girl. She regained consciousness before she died and cleared him, but it was time to change locations. There was a flurry of interest throughout Utah in uranium mining about that time, and Shoot-'Em-Up fell in line with it.

He had come from Kentucky to Colorado after he had been shot at and hit by numerous McCoys. He was badly crippled by gun-shot wounds long healed, one hip being nearly useless and one leg shorter than the other. His jaw was either partly shot away or "whickered around to one side" and his face was badly scarred. He was small, scrawny and grayhaired, and never any too clean. He wore the biggest hat he could buy, and a red handkerchief around his neck; instead of the usual Levis, he wore corduroy pants with the legs stuffed into his beat-up, run-over boots. He was the toughest looking character you ever saw, and wore his guns all the time. Wherever he lived he made trouble; he was mean and tough, and was always making someone "dance."

Shoot-'Em-Up was in with several local fellows on mining claims, he had mined some on the Henry Mountains, but he usually didn't stay long on a job. On a recent prospecting trip, he and his partner had borrowed some horses from Tomlinson, and he returned them all but Brock, a white horse speckled with liver-colored dots, saying he would like to keep Brock for a while. Bill didn't need the horse right then, so let him stay with Shoot-'Em-Up.

Usually the Tomlinsons wouldn't know the Pressetts had had a run-in with Shoot-'Em-Up-Bill until it was all over. There was about a half mile between houses across the fields, and more than a mile around by the road.

"What are we going to do?" Bill asked my father. "That man has got so bad we've either got to leave here or kill him— or let him kill some of us."

"Then kill the sonofabitch!" my father advised.

Lately, Tomlinson remarked, Shoot-'Em-Up was being particularly troublesome; he was drinking up the rest of the terrible pop-skull moonshine he had made and sold to the sheep shearers that spring, and he was more than dangerous. Although Bill Tomlinson didn't know it this evening, things were rapidly reaching a head.

That afternoon the two Cottrell boys had gone over after their saddlehorse which had strayed away, and as they passed Shoot-'Em-Up's dugout, he hailed them in. The boys were scared not to go, and he had got them drunk on his poisonous whiskey. The next morning, the two boys awakened before he did, and slipped away, sick and frightened.

When Shoot-'Em-Up missed them, he got on Brock and came over to the Pressett place, raving and cursing the kids for leaving and finally worked himself up to such a pitch he was taking in the whole family in his tirade. Mel slipped out the back window and came to tell his half-brother, Bill Tomlinson, what was going on.

Mel was so scared, that Bill and Jim Warner, Martha's brother who was staying with them, were alarmed. Jim grabbed his rifle and cut down through the fields afoot toward Pressetts'.

Bill's gun was at the corral on his saddle, so when he went to get it, he caught up a horse, jumped on bareback, and ran around by the road. It was about twice as far as Jim had to go, but Bill didn't save the horse any, and appeared on the scene just as Jim stepped around the corner of the house and Shoot-'Em-Up fired a shot at Jim, the slug hitting the ground between his feet and glancing harmlessly off.

When Bill and Jim opened fire, the outlaw whirled Brock and spurred him into a run into the brush and trees, shooting back. In front of Pressetts' was a wash, the old river bed; Shoot-'Em-Up disappeared into it just as my dad appeared on the scene. Remember, events had happened pretty fast, and since Bill didn't ask for help, my father was not going to take a hand. But when shooting started, he jumped the ditch in front of the house and ran across the field. He certainly wasn't a disinterested party, but he was a noncombatant, not even armed. Bill told him that Shoot-'Em-Up was over in the brush somewhere, as neither he nor Brock had come out of the wash, so my dad made a careful reconnoiter and discovered the outlaw in the wash, dead.

Pressett's brother went to Green River in a buckboard after the sheriff, Pete Riley. Frank Phillips came out with a car for the body and prisoners.

My father asked Bill if he had any money, and he said not too much, and Mama gave him a signed check to make out as he saw fit to procure a lawyer.

The coroner's jury, Len McCarty*, George Maggarrell, and Frank Butler, under Judge Turner, held the inquest in the McCarty store and after hearing testimony by the Pressetts, Jim Warner and Bill Tomlinson, pronounced the deceased had met his death at the hands of men defending their homes. In fact, Judge Turner reprimanded Bill severely for not doing it two years sooner, and remarked he ought to throw the book at him for his lack of civic pride in letting the matter drag on all this time.

When Bill returned, he handed the check back to my father with his thanks, and said it helped to know a man had friends back of him.

There is another little sidelight that I didn't know for years, but Shoot-'Em-Up had two valuable diamond rings that never came to light after the forces of law and order had visited his dugout.

We visited the Tomlinsons often after that, and when Bill moved his cattle to North Springs and built a cabin at Twin Seep around the ledges north of the main water, we often spent a day or two with them. They came to see us at the cabin at Crow Seep a few times. Bill never made it in the cow business; Martha hated living out on the range, and he finally moved his cattle above Sego coalmine near Thompson and worked in the mine. He had leased a few cows from my father, and he took them along—but that is another story.

---

*This has nothing to do with the story, but Len's father was Tom McCarty, a member of Butch Cassidy's Wild Bunch, who disappeared after the robbery of the Delta Bank in 1893. Tom's brother and nephew, Billy and Fred McCarty were killed in the robbery after they had killed the banker, Blachley. Tom never showed up again, but his two sons, Len and Lew lived in Green River for many years, where they ran saloons.

6

Developing the Home Range and Our Early Childhood

UNCLE OFFIE SPENT THE first
summer at the Roost, helping on the range. He and Papa
fixed up the Roost Spring, putting in new troughs. Aunt Jessie
(to be) must have been away visiting that summer because
Uncle Offie didn't meet her when he brought the wagon in
for planks to build troughs. This was the only summer Mama
didn't go to the Roost for the season; Hazel had been born in
February, and was just too little to take in camp.

The original troughs at the Roost had been put in by
Bernard when he was foreman for Buhr in the 1890s. He and
Joe Sylvester had fenced a plot thirty feet square where the
big spring gushed from the hillside, and gathered the water
into one stream running into two small troughs under the bank.

Jack Cottrell replaced Bernard shortly after marrying
Lida Ellen Tomlinson. He moved his new family to the Roost
where they lived in the cabin above the spring. Two or three
years later he was ousted by Jack Moore, who managed the
outfit until 1900, when Buhr sold out and left.

Over the original enclosure fence wild roses had grown
and hung over the trough and the corner of the fence. Two

cottonwood trees had sprung up, also, and the plot was rank with water grass and rushes. My father enlarged the enclosure and gathered the waters of the spring into a V-conduit, which sloped steeply into the waiting wooden troughs below the bank.

The old troughs were pretty badly decayed, and Papa replaced them, using three fir 2 x 12's, 16 feet long, with ends of the same plank material, held together with clamps (he called them "gripes") of scrap iron and long bolts. There were three of these bands to a trough, the strap iron tops and bottoms clamped tight by drawing up the nuts on the bolts. A partial partition in the center of the trough served as a brace under that band, and the troughs were placed too high for an animal to climb into. Later when Papa had a blacksmith shop, he modified these bands by making four long bolts with a loop in one end. These he could cinch down on planks three inches thick by eighteen inches wide and some twenty feet long, making troughs that have been in use for more than fifty years, and they are still sound.

The main Roost draw drained between the troughs and the ledge of the south side of the canyon not twenty feet away, but there was never much water in it; the thirsty sand above absorbed any flood or spring water before it got down to the troughs. The narrow space between the troughs and this towering ledge was a rock-paved standing place, always wet, always slippery, but no animal ever was injured on this hazardous looking apron. The ledge looked unsafe, and my father finally moved the troughs down the hillside away from the danger of this ledge toppling and mashing them.

The Roost Spring is bitter water. The Carmel formation around it is more liberally mixed with gypsum here than where it usually crops out between the Entrada and Navajo formations around the canyon rims of the Roost Country, and this gives the water of the spring a bitter taste. It is also impregnated with hydrogen sulphide and smells it! However, unlike

Dugout and other bad-tasting water of the San Rafael desert to the north, it has no bad effects on either men or livestock, and cattle and horses relish it and thrive on it. We called this Carmel formation "bad lands," as it was cut into deep gullies and sharp little hills which were hard to ride over.

One of the first range improvement projects must have been the Twin Corral Pond, since I can remember it as long as I can remember anything. Uncle Clyde Scharf, in age between my mother and Uncle Offie, spent considerable time at the Roost, mostly winter times. Although he was involved with the farm on Utah Bottom during the growing season, in late fall and early spring he was available and we always needed help.

Uncle Clyde was a real menace to cowpunching, being left-handed both in practice and policy. He confused the horses, trained to turn certain ways during roping or other maneuvers, by demanding the opposite action, and he was bullheaded and unreasonable.

Handling a team and scraper, however, presented no problems. The work horses were the bigger saddle horses, and how many, many miles must Babe, Prince, Pet, Dan and the others of the first few years at the Roost have traveled around and around between the depression being scooped out and the dam where the earth was piled to make the Twin Corral Reservoir.

A slip scraper holds about three bushels of dirt when heaped up well. It is dragged face down behind a team, and when the time to load comes, the driver (who has tied the lines together around his shoulders, and handles the team mostly by commands) grabs one handle of the scraper and tips it back. It is then a sort of scoop, pulled by the bail hooked into each side. He grasps the other handle and stooping, guides the sharp edge of the front into the ground while the team steps ahead steadily. When he has gouged up enough fill, he presses down on the handles, tipping the scraper back out of the ground, loaded. This load is skidded to the top of the dam, dumped by lifting a handle until the front edge catches, when a sharp heave throws the scraper on its face again.

The railroads of the West were built by slip scrapers until the Fresno came along. It could transport dirt longer distances much easier, because it traveled on skids on each side, rather than on the bottom as did the slip. The slip was handier for short turns and cramped spaces and took only one man and a team, while the Fresno required three or four horses and two men, (although the loader could load a string of Fresnos that were then dumped by the drivers). We had a slip scraper for a long time, but finally managed to get a Fresno, but the fun was gone out of "farming" for me by that time. I had followed the slip a good many miles, myself, loving the smell of the damp earth; the slip was somehow more intimate and friendly than the built-for-production Fresno.

Corrals were as important as watering places. There was a small one at Twin Corrals in the north end of the long draw that reached up from the pond (although it drained below the reservoir until we cut a ditch around the point of a hill and brought the water from this valley also into the reservoir). This corral was situated at the upper point of the valley, just before the breaks of Horseshoe Canyon dropped away into the heads of the canyons. It was not particularly well placed either as to location or ease of corralling. It was too far from the pond, requiring almost half a day to drive up to it from there, and cattle resisted always. They spilled around the wing end or back over the riders before being forced along the wing until the bulge of the corral was reached and the chute thus formed funnelled them through the gate. This drive was not entirely a waste, however, it mixed the cattle up well and promoted the following year's calf crop.

This was a "brush" corral, i.e., trees cut and piled into a

drift, trimmed of limbs on the inside. It was round in shape, with a gate closed by pole bars, and when enlarged was one of the main corrals for years.

Where the timber was thick, these were the most common corrals; through the years Papa built this kind at the Gordons, Hans Flat and on the Spur. At Crow Seep and the Roost, where the cedars were not thick enough, or were absent altogether, he built stockade corrals of posts set in the ground.

The corral on the Spur was one of the earliest ones, and it was a doozy! Papa had planned to approach it from the water hole, the Big Tank, a half-mile or so away in the canyon below, but it didn't turn out that way in practice. From that direction a low rim acted as wing. Instead of coming up across the little cedared flat, the roundup herd usually came over the top from the range on the Spur, and hit that easy down slope with but one thing in mind—water.

After the herd was rounded up and started back, every returning step was a fight; and sensing no good intentions from the hazing riders, the cattle broke back down the flat or they beat the men to the narrow trails in the rock ledge wing. It was almost impossible to get a bunch into that corral without several break backs, and there were many disastrous general "spills." This did nothing to train the cattle in the right procedure or to dampen their free spirits. It was easier to round up a bunch on the range, or to hold them in the Big Tank for branding.

That first year my father let his cattle work around from the Spur to Twin Corrals and finally the Roost. He couldn't let his herd go back to the Roost Flats until they had had time to forget San Rafael; he had them here and he meant for them to stay. He was afraid of the Gordons for a year-round range; it was high country and until his cows had wintered a time or two in heavy snow, he was wary of a big loss.

In the big canyons of Horseshoe and the Spur, the tanks

were safe enough. The deep tanks in the steep narrow canyons around Twin Corrals were the ones he worked on first.

Twin Corrals, his best range, was surrounded by canyons on three sides. Happy Canyon chopped off the whole south side, the north side was bordered by the many little canyon heads of the Horseshoe system. On the west, Twin Corral Box, Coyote, No Man's and many lesser, un-named gulches drained into the Dirty Devil River. These were narrow and steep and had various sized tanks scooped out by rainwater floods. Some of these holes had sand entrances from the down canyon side, and as the water receded, the cattle could crunch through the gravel of the apron and follow it back to the last drop.

All of the rain water in this Carmel, Entrada and Navajo sandstone was blood-red from the sediment picked up by the floods. The sand settled out of the water, but the fine clay never did, although enough of it would deposit on the gravel of the tank bed to seal the sand agaist too much seepage. As the level of the water dropped, this fine clay cracked and curled up in a crackle pattern some inch or so across in flakes as hard as slate. When we were little, Hazel and I used to make dishes of this, burn them in the campfire, then wonder what we did wrong. They were never the quality of the shards we found everywhere on the range, which were the pottery of the ancient Indians. We didn't know that various other ingredients had to be added to the clay to make pottery.

In the pothole type tank, flood water whirled over ledges and gouged deep cisterns with straight sides. While these were full, cattle drank, but as the water level lowered, a cow, in stretching to reach it, might lose her footing and slip in. Not being able to get a foothold on the vertical edges, covered with slimy mud, she would swim around and around and finally drown.

My father had such a feeling for his cattle that he was heartsick when he found one dead in some foreseeable situation such as this. He felt personally responsible—he had failed. Such a loss from his small herd was considerable, but he always felt it far more deeply than the financial loss.

Some of these tanks he made into important water holes, and my earliest memories are of working on them. There was a season for this work—just before the summer rains when the water level was low. He spent his Junes for three or four years on the project. He could and did blast trails into other tanks any time of the year.

Papa filled the cistern potholes. He would pick a big cedar tree close by, chop it down and roll and drag it to the tank and topple it in, cutting limbs so that it went to the bottom. Then he piled all the rocks that he could rustle up on top of it. The tree broke up the currents of the flood water and stopped the scouring process. After silt had settled in and anchored the fill for the ages, these tanks never had to be filled or fixed again.

Of course, Mama, Hazel and I helped with this, and as it was in the hottest part of the summer, Mama tried to protect our skins from the burning sun and drying wind by making us wear sunbonnets.

Ever wear a sunbonnet? You can see a small arc straight ahead and that's all. That wasn't what we girls planned to look at, there was too much happening all around us.

Mamma has told me in after years that she was certain the last sunbonnet, containing a rock, sailed out into a tank of opaque red water into which my father was pushing rocks and trees to keep it from being a straight-sided trap for a thirsty cow. And let me admit for the first time, she was right; I remember it distinctly. And the fact that we went bareheaded the rest of the summer, and, being red-haired and fair skinned, I was a solid scab from cheek bone to cheek bone didn't make me regret the sabotage for an instant.

The next spring, on a trip to Green River, my father remembered he had been requested to bring back hats for his little girls for Easter. He picked out some boys' hats, good felt ones that he thought would last through the summer. When he returned, we little girls accepted them with reservations, but when our playmates twitted us about their inappropriateness for the occasion, it is said I brought mine back into the house and putting it on the table, remarked, "Here, take your damned hat." I settled for it, though, when we got to the Roost.

French Seep was the first spring developed from scratch. It came out of the south side of a gully in a grove of oaks, and the fine sandy soil was black and probably very fertile. The water rose in a marshy spot and overflowed, running down into the bottom of the draw for a short distance.

The north side of this gully was white, steeply sloping sandstone, cut by shallow trenches, with many cross-scorings. It rose for fully a quarter of a mile, barely too steep for a horse to keep his footing on.

My father rode in one day to assess what had to be done to Frenchy to develop it. Always observant, he noted that the sandy flat above the spring had been torn up in long gashes by a bucking horse. He looked across the wash, and there on the white rock were long streaks of hair, hide and burned hoofmarks coming into the branches of a dead piñon that had fallen against the sloping rock.

He scouted back up the trail on the south side and pieced together what had happened. He knew there were three or four head of wild horses running on the Gordons and watering at Frenchy. As they had come into water, a cougar had dropped onto the back of one of them, but apparently too far back to bite into the horse's spine.

The startled horse had bucked, then had run down through the oak grove, but couldn't dislodge the lion. He then frantically ran up the rocky slope, getting almost to the top before he fell and slid, leaving plenty of evidence on the white slope. When he slipped into the branches of the dead piñon, he had dislodged the lion and broke out of the tree too fast for the cat to get him again. The cougar had padded up the draw, knowing that he probably wouldn't get another chance at that water hole for some time. He was just a transient, going across the desert from one mountain to another, probably.

So close had my father been to witnessing this drama, that the oak leaves carried from the grove and scattered on the hot rock had not yet wilted. He estimated it couldn't have been more than twenty minutes or half an hour.

I remember his working on Frenchy; he brought a trough out from Hanksville on the running gears of the wagon. He cleaned out the spring, and today there are no oaks left above it, but I remember when there was a small copse there, the ground covered with rustling leaves.

After the soil was scraped away, the spring was found to bubble up out of a crack in the white rock. He built an enclosure of short but heavy logs into the bank above it, and roofed this with short logs. He didn't notch the logs very deeply, so the pen was livestock proof, but a man could slip through to clean the spring. The water was sweet and cold when the sand and leaves were scraped away, and it had welled up into the depression in the rock seam. It was well worth waiting for.

One of our earliest semi-permanent summer camps was on Hans Flat, the first year Hans Anderson worked for us. Having a full-time hired man took some of the pressure off the family and my mother appreciated it. She was not up to the gruelling hard work of riding long distances every day, and when he could, my father left her and us little girls in camp. But this was seldom, he needed our help too much to let us lie around all the time.

He loved my mother dearly, and wanted her with him all the time; he was willing to overlook her general disinterest to have her at his side. And, since there was no way to travel but on a horse, she rode, and she endured the discomforts to live where she was reigning queen. She was not unhappy, and my childhood was extraordinarily peaceful and happy.

In that day and age women embroidered; they were also adept at crocheting, knitting, tatting, and other handicrafts. We called it "fancy-work." In the early years on San Rafael, when there wasn't money for this hobby, she had crocheted sewing thread up into patterns and then ravelled them out and crocheted the string up again. She had books of patterns and worked methodically from front to back, making a scallop or two of each pattern. I remember the little tin box of these she still had around years later.

Every time a lady sat down, she took up her handwork and Mama was no different, it was the womanly thing to do, and satisfied a creative instinct. It also produced the endless doilies, tidies, pillow cases, tablecloths and other finery dear to a homemaker's heart. If a housewife had nice things, it was because she was energetic and made them. And she taught her daughters the arts as soon as they were able to hold a needle or shuttle. This was sometimes uphill work with Hazel and me; we preferred laying out cow outfits in the sand.

While she sat under a cedar tree crocheting, tatting or sewing, Mama often sang or recited to us girls. Mostly, she sang; the human heart craves music and she satisfied both her own desires and ours with her songs of *Red Wing, Streets of Laredo, Silver Bell, Silvery Colorado Wends Its Way, Pretty Quadroon* and other songs of the times.

She recited several poems when we importuned her enough. Our favorite was the *Star Planters,* which she had clipped from the pages of a magazine and memorized; although we loved the *Schmall Rid Hin,* also. This was after the Mother Goose phase.

It was always exciting fun time when she dropped her fancywork and started:

THE STAR PLANTERS

Them stars! Oh, how often I've laid on the prairie,
    An' watched 'em go sweepin' around,
My bronco a-dozin' beside me, an' nary
    A breeze nor a whisper of sound!

I've learned the main bunch in the heavenly ranches;
    There's Jupiter, Venus and Mars.
Religion? He don't know its primary branches
    What ain't been alone with the stars,

Some clusters is branded—The Dipper, The Lion,
    The Eagle, the Sarpint, The Bear,
The Horns o' the Bull, and The Belt of Orion
    And Cassie O'What's her-name's Chair.

But lots of 'em's mavricks, roamin' the ranges,
    Unclaimed by the herds in the sky,
No part of the big panorma that changes,
    From Winter to Summer—and why?

Well, mebbe it's gospel, an' mebbe he sold me
    But here's the whole story, at least,
That Big Chief Citola, the Navajo, told me
    The night of the Corn-plantin' feast.

When all the mountains was set in their stations,
    An' threaded with canyons and rills,
The Star-worlds, the last o' the mighty creations,
    Was layin' in heaps on the hills.

In masses of silver, of gold and of copper,
    All polished and shinin' and new,
Poured out on the granite like corn from the hopper
    Awaitin' their place in the blue.

Now, first came the Bear o' the Mountains, who faces
    The North, from his cave in the scours;
He lifted his paws to the Heavenly spaces,
    An' laid out his picture in stars.

Then over the peaks of the western dominions,
    The Eagle who battles the storm,
Flew up to the Heavens with star-dusted pinions
    An' printed the lines of his form.

An' next, that the tribes an' the nations should wonder
    The buffalo leaped into the sky,
The shag-headed Bison, whose bellow is thunder,
    Embazoned his image on high.

But now came the Coyote, so crafty and clever,
    A scalawag all the way through;
The yap-throated, critical varmint who never
    Is pleased with what other folks do.

Says he, "These stars was intended to brighten
    The uttermost reaches of Night,
But YOU go and use 'em in pictures to heighten
    Your glory; and that isn't right.

"Jest WATCH ME! I'll show you how stars should be planted!"
    An' he jumped in the glitterin' piles,
He kicked and he gamboled, he danced and he ranted,
    An' scattered 'em millions of miles!

So that's why they glimmer at sixes and sevens,
    Stampeded all over the Vault
A lasting disgrace to the orderly Heavens,
    An' it's all that Coyote chap's fault.

An' still you can hear him, the yelpin' Coyote,
    A-mockin' the stars in the dim
Of night on the Barrens, with yammerings throaty
    While they look reproachful at him.

Well, mebbe it's gospel and mebbe he sold me,
    But that's the whole story, at least,
That Big Chief Citola, the Navajo, told me,
    The night of the corn-plantin' feast.

After a while she would run down and send us back to
building cow outfits in the clean red sand, hunting arrowheads,

picking the lovely lupine, mallow, bleeding heart, sunflowers and bluebell, or playing house by the hour in rooms defined by lines of pebbles or marks in the sand.

Some of our miniature cattle ranches were quite elaborate, too, with corrals, waterholes and trails carefully laid out on the sidehill. We must have made miles of these "cow-trails" by pinching our thumb and finger tip together and printing tiny cow tracks in the clean sand.

I remember one time when Dunc Gillies was "repping" for the Wrench M, he showed us how to make cows and horses out of the clay from around the water tanks. This was an advancement in our landscapes, but came sort of late in life; we were too grown up to play cow outfit much any more.

It was at Hans Flat, too, that I did my first piece of embroidery, the summer I was six. This was a real, honest-to-goodness store-bought project, quite simple, a sofa pillow in red clover with green leaves.

The needle was slippery and hard to guide and the thread tangled, and I was impatient because I wanted to play cows and corrals with Hazel. The project had about reached an impasse when Papa took over. Anything he did was OK by us girls, and also by his wife. He carefully and painstakingly explained the *modus operandi* to me, working a leaf as he went along. The pillow was finally finished and put away as my first embroidery; it's probably around some place yet.

I was adept with my hands, and I learned to crochet before I was four years old. I can pinpoint this because of a traumatic experience.

We had gone to call on some friends one evening whom a relative who had just lost her husband and her little girl were visiting. While we played dolls, I decided her dolly needed a cape, and I asked for a crochet hook and some string and crocheted one. Her uncle had been watching us play, more or less putting in his oar from time to time, and he gave her a dime to give to me for the cape.

I was just delighted, and when we got home, I showed Mama the dime. Still under the cloud of the other woman's loss, and seeing a way to teach me charity to the bereaved, Mama made me take the dime back the next morning.

I protested furiously, pointing out that the uncle had given the little girl the money for that specific purpose, and that I wasn't depriving the family of anything, but we trotted the dime right back to the little girl. Rather than teaching me a lesson in charity, it almost destroyed my faith in free enterprise.

After the first two or three hectic years, life at the Roost settled down a bit, but my father spent his entire professional life just one step ahead of a thirsty cow. However, he had to have a headquarters, and my mother was fighting valiantly not to have it built at Blue John.

Puppies were such fun and an important part of our childhood. Hazel (with braids) and me with our hats full of puppies.

7

Home Is Where the Heart Is

THE IDEA THAT ROBBERS ROOST
is on a high, inaccessible mesa is only partly wrong. Note on
a map of Utah that the Green River flows roughly southeast
until its confluence with the Colorado, then they both swing
southwest, the Dirty Devil entering below Cataract Canyon
of the Colorado. Robbers Roost lies in that wedge-shaped
section, being the high country above the Ledge, with Under
the Ledge a median shelf between the inner canyons and this
high cliff barrier. The country slopes back west from the high
Gordons and Spur toward the Dirty Devil, which is not so deep
as the Colorado in relation to the Roost country on that west
side. These deep surrounding canyons are in the main inaccessible with only a few trails off into them, but the northern edge
of the Roost, between the head of Roost Canyon and Horseshoe
is all open desert.

Roughly, Horseshoe divides the Roost Flats from the
Spur, with the Head of Horseshoe reaching up to Twin Corrals.
From Happy Canyon on the south to the northern boundary is
some fifteen miles, while the lip of the Ledge on the Gordons
to the western edge of the Dirty Devil is some twenty miles,
making a chunk of country roughly over 200 square miles.

The ridges are topped by cedars and piñons, which increase in size and density as the altitude rises toward the Gordons where thick timber surrounds the grassy parks. The Roost flats are gently undulating long swales reaching up from the Roost Draw to the ridge dividing them from the Crow Seep upper flats, which are in turn divided from Coyote Draw and from the Twin Corrals by two high, rocky ridges, heavily cedared. A long, narrow neck leads from Twin Corrals to French Seep, heavily timbered but with small grassy parks. To the left is first the Horseshoe breaks and then the Spur country; finally the neck narrows between the head of Millard Canyon on the north and the long sweep of the Happy Canyon rim on the south. The high range swings south at Frenchy, and the Gordons lie around the head of Happy Canyon. Flint lies on the southern end of the Gordons, and beyond it is Land's End, which is aptly named.

On the bench beneath the Ledge and the inner canyons of the Colorado and Green lie Bigwater (Elaterite) Basin on the north, with Waterhole Flat and the Andy Miller country on around south and west. Horse Canyon drains Bigwater, and in its farther reaches includes The Maze. Some of this Under the Ledge country is included in Canyonlands National Park, and perhaps the rest of it should be.

We never did consider the High Part of the Spur as Robbers Roost country, the division being the ridge that separates it from the Head of the Spur. Tidwells had a cattle outfit on the High Part of the Spur and Chaffins used Flint, both outfits also using lower ranges. Tidwells claimed the bottoms along the Green River, and Chaffins ran livestock Under the Ledge from the Maze south around Land's End to the mouth of the Dirty Devil.

Cattle range on the Roost year round, but sheep used to spend only a few months there when snow provided water for them. In my childhood the snows were far too deep for sheep to winter on the higher ranges, but the last fifty years have been part of a deep drouth cycle and sheep can range it during the cold months. Also, the past few years not enough snow has fallen to provide water for them, so they no longer trail to the Roost for a part of the year.

This whole country is geology heaven. All of the formations from the Top Entrada down to the Cutler lie open for study between the Gordons and the confluence of the Green and Colorado Rivers. The Ledge is Wingate, as are most of the canyon walls, and below are the Chinle and Shinarump, both rich in uranium. Below these lie the rich red Moenkopi, then the White Rim and Cedar Mesa, which are Cutler formations.

Above the Wingate is the Navajo with Carmel, a nonconformity lying in lenses of deep reddish purple, and above them the Entrada. Although crossbedding occurs in most formations, it is especially beautiful in the Navajo and the rounding bulks of the Entrada, the latter eroding into holes through which the wind sometimes moans in the canyons.

Buttes stand everywhere, ranging in shape from a slender spire to a large, flat-topped mesa, with formations like Jack and His Family in Bigwater forming real landmarks. Observation Dome, rearing above French Seep, can be seen all over southeastern Utah.

One afternoon my father dropped over the ridge and rode north along the dividing cedared crest between Cyclone, Sunflower and the upper flats of Crow Seep (although it was not yet named) and the lower Under-the-Point grasslands, ever hunting water to utilize this fine grazing. He eyed the beauty of the scene spread before him and wished Tootsie had come along to see it; she always liked a view and this was an especially good one, he thought. He ran his eye down over the waving prairie to the Dirty Devil gorge on the west, then up the Burr Desert to the sharp bulk of the Henry Mountains. Beyond them and to the northwest, the Thousand Lake Mountains loomed hazily, and from this vast panorama the Muddy and Dirty Devil rivers drained to converge just below Hanksville, only about thirty-five miles away had he been a crow. Above Hanksville, in the valleys of the river, Factory Butte sat, huge, flat-topped, with the upper third vertical and the talus slopes fanning out in pleats to the valley below. It was similar, he thought, to the Flat Tops back on the San Rafael Desert, both typical of the banded red and pink crumbly Summerville Formation.

He rode into a wet place in a draw and eyed it critically, but it seemed to be more or less a wet-weather seep. He really didn't expect to find a large spring, although the high vast flats above and to the east should betoken an outlet of stored water along this dropoff ridge. The ridge swelled to a bald slickrock point, with sloping bare rock below. Even a reservoir site was not beyond his line of exploration.

The draw ahead of him looked promising, as it drained the rock slope above, and he rode over the bank. In the bottom, hidden by the trees and bushes along the sides, a little black horse stood pawing out a hole in the wet sand to get a drink.

Papa was right on top of the animal before either of them was aware of the other. The horse broke wildly for the open, with Papa crashing behind him, already spinning out a loop. They topped out of the wash onto level ground at a dead run, and the loop snagged the quarry.*

---

*When Uncle Offie left for Hanksville to keep his wedding date, he borrowed the black horse we had named Crow to pack on his wedding trip and honeymoon. Unused to hard roads, the young horse developed "splints," knots on his slim front legs covering cracks in the bone. This didn't damage him much, except it was unsightly and while my dad was no sentimentalist over a horse, he took good care of them; a sore back or other damage was an abomination to him. He never rode or used the horse again, and I remember when he traded it off. The new owner rubbed the legs with Caustic Balsam, the universal liniment, and set off the next morning for San Rafael. Crossing the desert, the bone of one leg, gave way, and the new owner had to shoot the pony.

After tying the horse up to a tree, my father made a trip back to the spring, looking it over carefully. He judged that an enormous amount of "fill" would have to be scraped out of the gully to expose the rock bottom, but this could be used to build a dam below for a reservoir.

When he returned the next day for the horse, he brought Mama along, and she was enthusiastic. This was more central to the rest of the range than Blue John, she pointed out, and did it ever have a view! For many years she watched the seasons come and go from this sheltered cove. In the summer the early sun often picked up white dots of antelope on the wide range below the cabin, while midday lighted the overwash of orange mallow that swept the valley like flame, and the sun always set beyond the cool distance of the Henry Mountains. Snow in winter only softened the landscape, giving way to the vibrant red sand of spring, frilled by the tender green herbage of a new season.

Because the little wild horse was jet black, we called him Crow, and the spring became Crow Seep. We moved right in and started developing this for a permanent location.

The first camp was south of the spring, just before the trail going out to the upper flats crossed the first patch of slickrock after dipping into a wash and then climbing a sand hill that was always a favorite arrowhead hunting spot. This upsweep was liberally sprinkled with flint, and we found that every rain or windstorm uncovered new evidence that an Indian arrowmaker had camped on that slope many, many moons ago.

My father was right about the work that had to be done to remove the dirt from the narrow rock draw. Cedar trees, catclaw, rabbit brush and sarvice berry had crowded into the wet spot, and their roots were intertwined right down to bedrock. The sand had to be plowed before it could be slushed out with a slip scraper, and plowing was a real two-man job, since the team had to be driven expertly and took all the attention of one man, while the other manipulated the plow. Every few feet the team had to be backed up and the plow extricated from a tangle of roots.

The first year saw the upper end of the wash cleaned out and we found the spring sweating out of the white sandstone, clear and sweet. My father carefully blasted a hole out that would hold a barrel or two of water, and never did figure a better way to handle it than just to leave it open. He turned the wash above the spring so that flood waters went on by, and we cleaned it often. When it was dipped out and cleaned, how good the first bucketful of water would be as we waited to dip it up cupful by cupful as it ran into the clean rock pocket.

That fall the camp at Crow Seep was moved north of the spring. Most of the trails came in from the south and west, and the cattle were too spooky to come in to water past a camp. The permanent site took this into consideration. The first building was over a little ridge from the pond.

My father stretched a tent and built a rough saddle shed near by, and under a big piñon tree set up a simple shop. The next spring he spent the early part of the season, April and part of May, rounding up the Scharf cattle on the Henry Mountains and bringing them home up the Angel Trail.

We girls had our own horse that summer, Yanaho, a little white pony. My father was afraid we might be caught in a stirrup and dragged, so we rode a saddle with no stirrups. It was just something to hang onto.

Another complication in transporation was Whiskers, the puppy Bill Tomlinson had given us girls. We hadn't had him very long when he felt the urge to nip Browney's heels, and that was an indignity Browney had no intention of allowing. He kicked the puppy and broke its front leg. This usually meant that the dog had to be destroyed, but loud was the wail of us little girls, and my father let us keep him.

Whiskers made the ride on the Henrys in a nosebag hung

over our saddlehorn. We were not expected to do much cowpunching, only to keep up with the outfit, and Mama kept a wary eye on us all the time. But it did free her and Papa to do more cowpunching, and I'm sure they appreciated that.

Uncle Offie and Aunt Jessie helped with the roundup and there was a kid along to break some colts and swing packs. Other riders from Hanksville came in for a few days, so it was a most enjoyable experience for us.

One of these Hanksville riders was Neilus Ekker, whose parents owned the store in Hanksville. He and his wife had some little boys about our age, and many years later, Hazel married Arthur.

Evenings around the campfire, Neilus sang to us and it was wonderful as he had a marvelous voice. He had been the sweetest singer of the whole country for years and years. When he was only a kid, he used to carry the mail from Green River to Hanksville, spending one night at the Frenchman's on San Rafael. All of the sheepmen managed their trips in for supplies to coincide with his stay there, and the night was spent listening to him sing the wonderful songs of that time. Some of them I have heard in the years since, but " 'Twas a Winter's Day" and "Sweet Sixteen" were truly Neilus' own.

The Scharf cattle we were rounding up had belonged to my two uncles, Clyde and John Scharf. They had leased some cows from my father and moved them to the vacated Starr Ranch on the south side of the Henry Mountains. They couldn't get along, and Uncle Clyde left the country, and Papa bought back the ranch and the cattle from Uncle John. There were a few tools, I believe the first anvil he used at the Roost came from the Starr Ranch, but I don't know what else. Mama found an old violin and brought it along.

My father had had all that fiddle he needed. Once before, early in the spring, a bunch of the fellows had been rain-bound a day or two in the cabin with nothing to do but play cribbage and kill time. Papa was fighting an attack of quinsey, and when first one then another would get bored with the cribbage game and saw a few untuned shrieks out of the fiddle, he, suffering on the bed in the corner of the room, would curse to himself. He never learned to play cribbage and the "fifteen-two, fifteen-four" of the counting always reminded him of this and infuriated him. But if Tootsie wanted that fiddle, she got it.

When I went to St. Mary's Academy several years later, I took violin lessons because we had an instrument on hand, but I wanted to play the piano, and didn't make much progress on the fiddle.

I remember the first Christmas we came home, Hazel had learned a piece on the piano and I on the violin, and we entertained the folks *ad nauseam.* My grandparents were down for dinner, and we were performing when my grandfather wandered out into the kitchen.

"Did you get tired of the music, Dad?" Mama asked him, and he replied:

"Yes, it reminds me of the Chinaman that got a job herding sheep. He stayed for only a few days then quit, and when asked why, said, 'Too much tinkle-tinkle—baa-a-a!' "

The fall of 1915 Mama was most reluctant to return to Hanksville. She kept saying she wouldn't and when the first snows of the season drove over the tent, her husband began to pay attention. Cutting cedar posts as fast as he could, he hauled them in and started putting up a cabin.

Everything Joe Biddlecome did carried the stamp of his four-square, honest workmanship—he couldn't do sloppy or ugly work. And he built no hut this time. Although there wasn't a cedar post long enough to reach the length of any wall of the 14' x 16' cabin, he laid up four strong walls, put down a pine-board floor, topped it all with a shingle roof. He put a window in each wall but the front, which faced east so that the prevailing winds from the south and southwest didn't blow in. The door would have been handier on the south, but much, much less comfortable.

There were several trees around the yard, a big piñon out front which sheltered the blacksmith shop and some small cedars in the back where Hazel and I set up our playhouse.

He nailed the last shingle on and moved us in the first day of November in a blizzard. Oh, the cozy joy of being in her own home, with her family warm and well—and the whole winter to do as she pleased. No longer did she have to conform to community mores she could neither understand nor approve. My mother was most content.

That year we girls were old enough to enjoy a Christmas tree, so we had one in all its glittering glory. However, Christmas was two days late. A heavy storm brought my father out with a pack outfit and a couple of strong, grain-fed horses to ride the Gordons and Spur and see how the cattle were wintering. He didn't return until the 27th, so we had Christmas then.

That winter, too, we began school work, learning to read and write. Lessons lasted until spring released us little girls out onto the rocks above the house and into the lovely, flower-studded sandhills.

As the last patches of snow melted under the trees, and the north sides of the knobs and south sides of the washes, the air was filled with the heady aroma of wet earth. The rock warmed, and we scampered over its bare, clean slopes, following it down to the draining crease, drank from the pools of pure snow water caught in the crack, and set up playhouses in the scattered rocks near the spring.

We were all home at last, and we enjoyed it to the full— we kept right on enjoying it for years and years.

The summer my father and Uncle Offie built the Hans Flat Corral they used the mare Pet to drag in the trees. We played with her colt, and my mother took a picture with Hazel pretending to mount up while I held the horse.

Branding a colt; note how the feet are tied, which is different from the way a cow's feet are tied.

8

Horses

WHEN MY FATHER WAS about twelve years old he ran away from home and went to live with the Swaseys. Although a polygamous family, they were outside of the somewhat hysterical fanaticism of the church, and their broadminded attitude was balm to this overchurched waif. The stories that he told of the Swaseys were vivid and wonderful, but those men were horsemen born and bred, and they passed on their beliefs and skills to him. The basis of their philosophy was that in thinking, in judgement, in action, a man and his mount moved as one. These men didn't have to remember to care for a horse—any horse—it was an instinct. Being cast in that mold himself, and growing through his formative years in such an environment, Joe Biddlecome became almost brother to the horse.

The country was full of wild horses, descendants of those turned on the range or that had escaped from parties or from ranches. The few remaining at the Roost were probably from the fine stock Buhr had raised there in the 1890s. The vast San Rafael desert carried possibly thirty bands altogether at the time we moved to the Roost. Some of these had good bloodlines, and when caught and put under saddle, made fine mounts.

These desert broomtails watered along the San Rafael, at Tanks of the Desert and in the southern reaches of their range at North Springs as well as at Keg Springs on the eastern fringe of their range. Along that curving shelf that begins at North Springs, runs north and then bends west until it peters out near the Flat Tops were numerous rain-water tanks. On the north flank of this ridge, Sweetwater seeped a niggardly flow.

In the interior of this vast plane of high sand bumps, oak knolls, long sand swales and blackbrush ridges between Sweetwater and the San Rafael, Dugout flowed freely a few miles of bitter alkaline fluid that, while it didn't seem to bother horses and cattle, acted as instant purgative to man. The saying was that if you felt *you* had to take a drink, never use a cup; you couldn't possibly set the cup down and get your pants off in time!

It was these desert horses that my father always said kept him going until he could get started in the cow business. He even ran one bunch out on the top of the south Flat Top and caught a half-grown colt out of it. He could catch a horse and break it in his ordinary routine, selling it for five or ten dollars for another grubstake. I once heard Dunc Gillies agree that "it must have been about horse time again when I stayed overnight in your camp that time."

While these horses were *instant grubstake,* they passed through his hands so rapidly that they often didn't receive a name until their ultimate owners bestowed one. But his basic "saddle string" remained the same, and was composed of really fine horses—Browney, Fan, Pet, Prince, Babe. My earliest memories are of riding behind my parents on one of these.

Browney was out of Penny a little mare Mama's parents

had given her for a wedding present. What Browney's sire was is a question that never came up, just as Penny's antecedents were not of much importance, but he was no ordinary horse. Moab was famous for its fine saddle horses, Booger Red having gone to Texas to help propagate the quarter horse type; Browney could well have been out of a fine stallion.

He was bigger than the average saddle horse of the region, deep chested, flat thighed, trim legged and with the shrewdest look in his big, full eye that you can imagine. When he was a colt, my father put a "wineglass" brand ᗄ on him with a calf iron, "big enough to rattle in the brush." This was to be our horse brand, but when he moved, someone was already running it, and Browney was the only one that ever carried it.

Although he was big enough, Browney never suffered the indignity of being used for a draught animal as Babe, Pet, Prince and others of his brethren were. He was king of cowhorses of his time and he received the proper homage.

In the early years my mother was often called upon to "make a hand" and mounted on Browney she could do it; she kept him from getting bored and wandering off, and he did the work, usually of cutting out the steers for the yearly cattle drive to market at Green River. Steers just looked different from heifers to my father, but to my mother the only difference was that steers had tassels on their bellies, and given time, she could pick them out. However, in the fast shuffle of the cut she didn't have time to look. After trimming the grown cattle out of the bunch, this last separation of the yearlings got "hairy" until my father figured out a sure-fire system: He hit the animal he wanted out with the loop of his lasso, and the mark showed on the dusty hide. These, Browney let out of the gate as they were cut to him, and he held the rest (mostly!) back. When the action got too fast, it was about all Mama could do to stay with her mount, doing little in the way of guidance. Browney was tolerant and learned to dodge back under her and keep her topside, as well as to watch and handle the cattle.

Very early in the business Fan was added to the cavvy.* She was a big black mare mule that became almost a legend in the country. She was gentle to a point, although she was not broken to saddle, being far too valuable as a pack mule. And she never was worked in harness, either.

Fan and my father understood each other perfectly. In those early days, there was really no permanent camp and every morning the gear was packed on a mule and taken along. It took only a few minutes to throw the grub and utensils into the pack bags, saddle Fan and hang these on, throw the bed over the top and tie it all down with a diamond hitch. Then Fan's lead rope was tied to the pack and she was forgotten until night. She followed the riders or she wandered quietly among the cattle they were driving. When night came, my father had only to step off his horse by a tree and Fan was there ready to be caught and unpacked.

My father had perfect rapport with all his horses, but particularly with Fan and Browney. There was no nonsense between him and them, he didn't pamper or fool with them; he respected each one and ruled with a strong, purposeful hand. They respected him, too, and there was trust and liking between them and him. I can well remember that when the nosebags were filled with oats, which we usually fed to supplement the restricted grazing of hobbled horses, there was never a nosebag for Fan. Instead, Papa would roll down the grain sack and set it in front of her. She would eat as much as she wanted and wandered off—a horse would have gulped down this concentrated feed and foundered himself. This was a sort

---

*The Spanish word *cabello* is pronounced ca-vi-yo, and I am sure that is where we got our word for the horses in the active saddle string, as opposed to the ones running on the range.

of grandstand play that was used to impress the visitor and it always did!

I don't know how we could ever have survived at the Roost without Pet, the big bay mare with the nick out of one ear. Mama rode her for the first few years because she was gentle and steady. She was also used to break green broncs to harness, and she mothered a whole cavvy of horses. Her horse colts, Napoleon and Buffalo, partook too much of her Percheron ancestry to be good saddle horses, but her mare colts, Mayflower and Iroquois crossed with the lighter strains we had for herd sires, produced many, many good colts.

I remember when Pet got the nick taken out of her ear, although I couldn't have been more than about three. She and Browney had a fight, and I remember how scared Mama was, and how Papa wouldn't let anyone interfere. The horses were fighting in the narrow lane of the road that ran from our place in Hanksville up to town, and the battle was noisy and bloody. Both horses screamed as they rose and struck at each other, hoofs thudding on bodies, then they fell apart, came together kicking and biting. It was a real war, and when the battle ended in a sort of armed truce, they were both exhausted and bleeding from dozens of tooth and hoof wounds, although the only permanent damage was part of the end of Pet's ear, which Browney had bitten out. Browney never challenged her reign again, and she never bothered him. This is the only instance I have ever known of a fight between a mare and a gelding—a fight to the victory.

Prince was a gray horse with the Swasey *Pine Tree* brand ⋔ on his shoulder. I don't remember anything particular about either him or Babe, a red roan, except that they were good, honest horses and did a lot of work. They were used both as work horses and saddle horses, although neither of them excelled in the latter field.

Horses in the cavvy were hobbled to keep them close to

camp; that is, their front feet were tied close together.

The first hobble a colt wore was made from a gunny-sack. The sack was opened, laid out flat, folded corner-wise once then from the apex of the triangle, it was laid in about three inch folds to the long side. This long fold was split for about six inches in the center, one end run through the slit, making a long string.

This bulky string was placed around the right front leg of the bronco as the man knelt or squatted by its front leg. Three or four twists were tightly made and the two ends brought around the left leg and tied in a square knot. Until the colt learned to jump with both front feet at the same time, he could skin himself up pretty badly with leather hobbles, but by the time he had worn out a sack, he had the hang of the thing, and could be trusted with leather.

Chain hobbles were two leather "cuffs" connected by a chain six to ten inches in length. To release these, one cuff could be unbuckled and then buckled on the same leg with the other, which left that whipping chain to bang up a horse's feet and legs, or the hobble could be entirely removed. The burden of some fifteen or twenty pairs of these was considerable, so we used strap hobbles, mostly.

Strap hobbles were long strips of leather with a buckle on one end and two loops—either strips of leather riveted to the main strap in strategic places to "space" the horse's legs, or there were regular gadgets for this use. After taking these off the horse, they were fastened around his neck where they remained until they were again needed, whether or not the horse was ridden that day.

Horses were *never* driven with the hobbles on, although catching them on the open range was sometimes a good trick. Usually, if one of them resisted, a good run with the loose horses showed him the error of his ways and he stopped to be turned footloose.

After Roy Dickerson came to work for us, strap hobbles lost some of their handiness. Little Dick always sneaked right up to a horse's hobbles, never looked the horse in the eye at all, but kept his gaze on the hobbles. Even a bronc would let him right up to its feet, for some reason, never spooking if it thought Dick had some other goal than its sensitive head. The old horses soon learned this, too, knowing they were not really caught until something was placed around their necks, and they got so they wouldn't let a man rise up and put the hobbles on their necks. The wrangler would be stuck with four or five or a dozen extra pairs of strap hobbles buckled around his wrangle-pony's neck when he brought in the cavvy.

Horses were never hobbled at Crow Seep; it was home. A night horse was kept up, and just before dawn, the wrangler (or jingler, as we sometimes called him) saddled and set off past the spring, around under the ridge, at a long lope. Although this ridge was not much of a barrier, there was plenty of room in the flats below it and the horses grazed there. By the time the jingler got out to where the farthest horses grazed it was light enough to see and he started them in, picking up the rest as he came along.

Horses are handled differently from cattle; you just can't hurry a cow, but if you don't drive horses at a good swinging trot at least, they scatter and graze. So the cavvy comes in on the run with a whooping Comanche popping a stinging hard-twist off the rumps of the slow or lazy. The fun of riding fast in the cool dawn was worth getting up early to jingle; I liked to do it and usually did.

Horses do a lot of fighting among themselves, and they finally develop a pecking order. A cavvy that's driven a few days soon strings out in about the same order, and when turned loose, the horses divide off in about the same small groups each time. There will be several bunches of two or three or five or six scattered over the flat, grazing. When the sun comes up and they shade up for the day, two will stand head and tail and switch flies off each other.

If we bought a horse from, say, around Price, then a year or two later bought another one from the same area, they buddied up, even if they were not from the same ranch or had never seen each other before. This happened so many times that we didn't think it could be by coincidence at all; it pointed to communication.

We never trimmed our horses' tails. It was not the fashion to do so when I was young, and in my memory I can still see the extreme grace of a working cowhorse as his tail swept and swung while he dodged and turned with the cow he was handling.

When I was nine and Hazel seven, we each got our own horses and saddles with stirrups. Now we were expected to take our places on the day's circle and make a hand, and we lived all summer on horseback. Papa never expected this of Mama; she rode, but not with the skill or enthusiasm of us girls.

My horse was Darkey, a gentle, but handy cowhorse, and Hazel's was Tom Mule. The next winter Papa "necked" a desert wild colt he had roped to Tom Mule and they ran along the side of a ridge covered with ice and snow and slipped and fell one on each side of a big sarviceberry bush and both strangled to death. The next summer, Eph Moore wandered past and we bought Mickey and Navajo from him. Mickey was a little blue roan, a typical Indian pony, but his pertness and cuteness became almost a legend, and Hazel loved him dearly. He was her special mount for years.

Darkey had one habit that caused me bitter despair— he was bridle shy. If the bridle bit so much as touched a tooth, he held his head up so high I had to have help to get the bridle on him.

My father had showed me how to hold the bit; he used bits with open loops—never spade bits—so that a horse could fall and do no damage to his tongue. I have seen horses with awful scars on their tongues from a bar or spade bit.

The trick was to take the bit in your left hand, while you held the top of the bridle over the side of the horse's nose so he couldn't turn away. If he backed and turned away, a rein hooked over his neck and held also in your right hand, stopped him. You held the bit with your index finger in the bit loop, your thumb on one side and your middle finger on the other. You pried the horse's mouth open with your middle finger and thumb, and with your index finger slid the bit down the thumb and middle finger, without its ever touching a tooth, pulling it up by the headstall, too. By the time my hand got big enough to bring this off, I had graduated from one horse to a string, and I often saw riders look at me strangely when I bridled a horse so expertly.

I had learned in a hard school; if I handled Darkey carefully and didn't touch his teeth with the bit, we got along fine in the morning when we started out, or during the day when I stopped to give him a drink at a waterhole. (We watered our horses every chance we got, and we took the bit out of their mouths so that they could get a good drink, and also let them rest a few minutes.) When a grownup would come upon me cursing and furious with Darkey holding his head toward the sky, it made me pretty careful with him for a good long while. It was humbling to have to be helped with so simple a chore as bridling my saddlehorse.

About this time my father was beginning to find that he would have to raise his own saddlehorses. Passing riders were bringing in a few, some of which returned to their old ranges as soon as green grass came in the spring, and often we never did get them back. We had more crew to mount up now, too, with one or two hired men as a rule, particularly during the riding season from steer-gathering in the early spring on through branding until bull-gathering in the fall. And we girls had to have two or three horses in a string to keep mounted up, with another string resting on the range. Mama still rode Browney, Button, or in the later years, Red Fox.

The first stud we bought for the Roost was a bay, one-eyed horse we got from Bill Tomlinson—a well bred animal and a real herder. We had several mares then, and were having our troubles. As soon as spring began to fill every horse with green grass, they felt so gay they became wild desert stallions. Each one started "herding" a mare or two, not letting any other horse near her. So they fought and bit chunks out of each other's backs which kept them out of the saddle strings. Too, they scattered from the cavvy and we spent needed cow time in hunting horses.

And the mares got sassy—they didn't want to run together and they didn't want to stay where we put them. Consequently we lost two or three that wandered north to Antelope and down past North Springs where they were gobbled up by desert studs and never allowed to come back.

Goodeye put a stop to all this. He was corral raised, but unbroken and four years old when we turned him loose at Crow Seep. He started with the mares at hand, and soon taught them their manners. Because of his disability, he close herded and he herded *mean*. When he laid back his ears, stuck his head out and bowed his neck, he was the most vicious looking animal I ever saw—he was wickedness personified.

One day I remember he brought his bunch from watering in the pond back east of the cabin, headed out the road to Sunflower Valley. The mares wanted to drop down by the corral, but he wanted them to go on past, and hit the road up the draw. He made a pass along that side, but the mares still had ideas and scattered behind him. He came back, and they must have thought there were six of him; he tore off hair from one set of ribs and hips and another till the air was full of it and the humbled mares were going his way and glad to do it.

As Goodeye ran onto a saddlehorse with a mare, he took her and left a much chastened former harem leader, considering himself just a plain old saddle gelding again. Sometimes it took months to heal his ripped hide and the battered ribs and banged legs, but one application cured him, he never quit the cavvy for cafe society again. And the mares grazed in a bunch under discipline and in peace.

The next stud (we were never allowed to use that word, we had to say "stallion" for some prissy reason) was Zebra Dun, and thereby hangs a tale. Colonel Tasker came into the country during the Green River boom, about 1906 or 1907. His interest was oil and mining; seems he was a promoter as he didn't actually own any wells or mines. His eldest son, Harry, was enamored of the West and got some horses together somewhere, leaving them in Millard Canyon. The story is that he started to the Roost with them, but Uncle Offie ran onto him before he had a chance to turn them loose, and "helped" him take them on across the range into Millard Canyon.

A few years later, Harry was talking to Papa one time and wished he was rid of those horses. Papa gave him $100 for the "Long-H" brand ├────┤ and we got ready to round 'em up.

By that time, Lou Chaffin of Rabbit Valley, above Hanksville on the Fremont (Dirty Devil) River had moved his cows to the Bigwater country off Under the Ledge from the Gordons, his boys taking care of them. There were wild horses Under the Ledge, too, left there originally by Butch Cassidy and the Wild Bunch.

Lou used to tell about two gray mares, a year apart in age, but apparently sisters, or at least half-sisters, that had been left in Horse Canyon. Tom Baker from Wayne County found out about them and went down and brought them out. They were then three and four years old. He broke them to drive and turned them in on his grocery bill; the grocer drove them to Richfield where someone fancied them and he sold them for $200, a fabulous price for horses in those days. They spent the rest of their lives as a fancy buggy team for one of the church (Mormon) officials in Salt Lake City. I was never interested enough in the story to trace down the names, but I don't doubt the truth of the story.

The Chaffin boys had caught some of the horses Under the Ledge, but there were still some around in the canyons that had never reached Millard Canyon where the Tasker horses were.

This was the summer I was fifteen and Hazel was past thirteen. Mama and Papa put an outfit together and started down to round up those horses, just the four of us. At the time there was an oil rig of the old cable-tool vintage drilling a well at French Seep. It ran periodically for several years, with T. C. Conley promoting it. He would come in with funds, hire a crew who would drill until the money ran out and then a while longer; the men would quit and he would have to shut down and go back to the midwest and get some capital together. He was a most persuasive man, and always seemed to get a few thousand dollars together to reopen the rig.

One time, he used to tell, he was too broke to buy anything but several rolls of wallpaper which he picked up in a sidewalk stall for practically nothing, and a couple of lumber crayons. He borrowed an office from a friend, called together some men with money and gave them a lecture in geology of the west, drawing charts on the wall paper, tearing off one section and starting another all afternoon. He got his capital.

Mrs. Conley spent considerable time at the rig, usually doing the cooking, but she was really a finely cultured city girl and it was hard work for her. Her brother and his wife spent several months there the summer we gathered the Tasker horses.

Since Conley made arrangements to buy some of the overflow of French Seep with which to drill his well, we got acquainted with them, and we all found much to admire in each other. We used to take Mrs. Conley horseback riding, although we couldn't see why she thought it was such a treat. We admired her greatly.

We stopped to have dinner with them this day, then went on down North Point and dropped down the North Trail into Big Water (Elaterite) Basin. I don't remember where we picked up the Chaffin boys, but we did, and went around above the rim of Horse Canyon on a trail just wide enough sometimes to get a horse between the ledge and the lip of the canyon. We met Eph Moore and his nephew, Cole Allred, on the Green River and Bill Moore, Eph's brother, was with us for a day or two. All this extra help depleted our groceries to the point that it looked like a good idea to go deer hunting.

The boys found an old boat and went across to the next bottom, and some of them hunted on our side of the river. They wasted the day; no one got a deer and Fawn Chaffin ripped his shirt all off crawling through the willows on the deer trails of Valentine Bottom.

Fawn was redheaded, with that skin that does not really tan, but only burns and blisters. My father took off his outer shirt and gave it to Fawn, together with his watch, since his undershirt didn't have a pocket. Why my father carried a watch is a mystery; we lived by the sun anyway, but he did. After Fawn got the watch, we would ask him the time to hear him extol the merits of the watch—it regulated the sun and stars and so forth—for some minute or so of pompous oratory, while he held it for exhibit. It was often returned to the pocket without being consulted for the time, but by then we had become so enthralled we didn't care, either.

We collected a few horses, and some got away. During the trip Eph returned a horse he had taken a year or so before to break. This was a horse we had gotten from Uncle Offie and it carried his TJS brand $\mathcal{J}^5$ on the jaw. Fred was promptly put into my string, and he was a dandy. He was well broken, handy on a rope, and altogether a good, honest horse. My father was so impressed with the job of breaking that he had Eph come back to the Roost and get six head of young horses to break. He wanted to do it, since he had Cole to help him.

We never knew who did the job, but the horses were returned to us all ruined. Millard was bedrocked—that is ridden until he completely gave out and never recovered from it. He always jog-trotted, never regained a springy, easy gait, and he never had any life. Silvertip was cold jawed; he fought a bridle bit so bitterly that he wasn't good for anything, and he looked always for a chance to kill his rider. I rode him for years, but he had to be watched every second, and never trusted. Spareribs had big lumps on his ribs, probably from their being cracked by kicks from another horse, so he couldn't be used.

I can't remember what we called the little red roan horse that my father thought would make such a good saddle horse. One morning in Horseshoe Canyon, he threw his saddle on this pony, mounted and started gathering cattle down the canyon. Hazing some cows down out of the rims, a difference of opinion arose, and Papa tried to make the horse do something. The little pony had a fit; bucking and fighting his head blindly, he ran out on a slickrock dropoff and slid over the edge into Horseshoe killing himself. My father just managed to save himself, but he was heartsick for months over the accident. Had he known the horse had these fits from panic and fury of mishandling, he would never have ridden him in so dangerous a place. The others I don't remember, perhaps only these were returned, but it seems to me he got six head.

This was rather a poor showing. It is an old range saying

that you get one out of five from good range run colts. You lose one from some infection or accident, one never really breaks gentle, and of the remaining three, two are just so-so, run-of-the-mill horses, and the last one is worth all the bother and failure of the other four. But four failures out of six, or six out of six, is a rough deal.

Zebra Dun was garnered with a mare or two and we brought him home for a stud. A big bay horse, he had a long mane and tail, and looked good. But he was nothing but a blowhard. He wouldn't or couldn't herd, and by this time the mare bunch numbered fifteen head and we needed a herder badly. I don't remember what became of him, but our next stud was Happy Jack.

Some years before my father had bought in on a stud shipped in from Kentucky. Papa had nothing but contempt for Becluse when he saw him—he was a helluva looking piece of horseflesh with one defect that no amount of registration in the Jockey Club stud book could gloss over, his ankles (or pasterns) were so elongated as to be almost a deformity. Without good feet a horse was a total loss, and my father used his stud privileges with Becluse only once. Pet produced Iroquois, who didn't carry this fault.

In fact, most of his colts didn't have this failing, not finding a corresponding gene in the mares, probably. As I have done a bit of digging for material on Becluse, I am beginning to learn he was a really outstanding animal. Throughout Emery County, much of Wayne and the north end of Grand, slopping over into the Uintah Basin, his line is still the best bunch of horses around. Jim McPherson owned him his last few years, and the McPhersons and Wilcoxes value his colts highly.

In Green River, Pete Riley drove a little smooth chestnut sorrel buggy mare, and he bred her to Becluse. She foaled a sorrel colt with a blaze face, a nice, smooth colt. Somehow Pete never got around to altering the horse, but traded it to the Herron boys. They broke it, and when it was about three years old, one of them rode to the Roost.

Clip Charlesworth was working for us, and he and the Herron boy got to bragging and matched a race with Clip's mare and this colt. She had just foaled, but they measured off about what they figured would do it, down in the hardpan flat below the cabin at Crow Seep, and with me up on the sorrel horse, ran a race. The mare beat, but the Herron boy couldn't take the razzing and bet a hundred dollars for a race in Green River in thirty days.

Clip knocked a hundred-dollar colt in the head and started training the mare, and he knew how. When he showed up for the race, she was in perfect condition, but the sorrel colt was a long way from racing trim. He was thin and spiritless. They pulled his heavy shoes and put on racing plates, but he still got beat—he just wasn't as fast as the mare, a fact I had maintained all the time.

When he got beat that time, the fellow was amenable to a deal, and we bought Happy Jack for $200. The horse needed care, and we didn't need him until the next spring, so my Uncle Alex, Papa's half brother, took him to the Last Chance ranch at the mouth of Price River to feed over the winter, hoping he would develop a little spirit as he put on some fat.

We went up to get him the next spring, and he had spirit all right. Mama rode him to Green River, and he never quit fidgeting or trying to bite or kick some other horse all the way down the river. He was a raving beauty, and we called him Happy Jack.

He herded after a fashion, but we accused him of laying out a mare for bait so he coult beat the b'-jasus out of a saddlehorse, instead of keeping his house in order. He fought for the fun of it, and he was mean. He even got so he'd take on a rider mounted on some particular horse he had it in for, and he suffered several severe hardtwistings as a result. We never handled him at all without a rope down, ready for use. He sired several colts, the sorrel ones not worth a damn, but every colt that was bay or brown made a fine saddle horse.

After my father's death, Mama leased him as well as the mare bunch to Art Murry and Happy Jack finished his life on the range between the Green and Colorado in Dead Horse Point area. He sired some good colts over in that country, too.

While Happy Jack was reigning at the Roost, the horse business received a stunning blow from an unlooked for direction, and it never recovered. Several years before my father had leased some of his surplus cattle to Bill Tomlinson, who had taken them to the mountain above Sego, when he took a job in the coal mine. When Papa wanted his cattle back, Bill wouldn't ante. They were old friends, so there wasn't much really said. Bill merely remarked if he wanted 'em, he'd have to come and take them away from him, and my dad opined as how he might do just that. Bill thought the cattle were on a range unknown to my father, and he could keep him from gathering them.

Papa let the matter settle until early spring, when he and Rod Swasey left Green River, each leading a spare horse, but without a pack. They weren't going on a camping trip, but you can take my word for it, they were well mounted.

By the next morning, they were at the back edge of Bill's range, and that day they quietly seeped down through, gathering the forty or so head of cattle due. That night they brought them out through a strange country down mountainsides cut by canyons crossing the Green River on the bridge just before daybreak. At sunup, the sheriff of Grand County was waiting on the bridge to head them off; Bill had learned of the raid and called the law. If he had been a couple of hours earlier, he could have claimed the cattle and by a lawsuit at least postponed their removal. However, when the cattle were out of the county and back in my father's hands, with his brand still on them, Bill had to call it quits.

Rod Swasey leased the cattle, and when it was time to pay the lease, he talked my father into taking 33 head of yearling, two and three-year-old mules.

Papa took Black Bess, a fine mare he had bought from Lou Chaffin, and went to Green River to receive the mules. Rod helped him bring them to the Roost early in the spring. It would be hard to say how much those mules cost him, and how many calves and colts they killed before he shipped them to Kansas City to the mule market the second fall. They were as wild as jackrabbits and not much bigger. The bunch was easy enough to handle, as they followed Black Bess closely. When we corraled them, one or two of the older ones would break back, run up on a hill and stand there and trumpet, upsetting every horse's nerves in earshot—and that must have been miles. The ones in the corral milled like wild-eyed furies, crowding close to the bell mare with Bess laying into them by tooth and hoof in every direction, while her colt cowered between her front legs.

When they were gone at last—ah, peace! It was wonderful at the waterholes with that horde of giant lice no longer abominating the countryside. But the mare bunch was in such a mess that Papa never got it all sorted out again before he died, and Mama leased them to Art Murry together with her cattle from the estate.

Although we worked horses much less than cattle, they were lots more fun. Half the pictures we have are of handling horses and actually the time involved wouldn't have been more than 5% of the actual work time at the Roost.

There are two ways to get an unbroken horse thrown down, one to frontfoot it and the other to rope it around the neck and choke it down. Frontfooting can lead to a broken neck in the fall, and there's not always a man catty enough to grab the head and yank it up before the horse gets on his feet again.

Although I never saw a horse choked to death, choking one down is exciting. The instant the horse's eyes glaze and he collapses, the rope must be loosened. He heaves in great draughts of air, and by the time he gets enough strength to struggle, his front feet are tied together, a loop run between them and the top hind foot pulled up. It is almost impossible to break a cow's leg in tying it down, but because a horse is so much stronger, it is well nigh impossible not to damage his legs by handling him.

Holding an animal down while adjusting ropes or tying it differs with the animal. Horses get up head first, then front feet; therefore, in holding one down, you tip his nose up, but you put a knee in his neck so he can't raise that up. If you hold his head up too far, he turns over and while you are discombobulated by this maneuver, he jumps up onto his feet —right in your middle. So—*pull back on that nose, push down on that neck* and be ready to get away fast if he is too strong or too quick for you! Watch those hind feet, too!

Colts were castrated at three or four years of age, rarely before, as they have to reach maturity. Just as Mama would never allow us to use the word stud, this operation was not nice, so the secret rite was not witnessed by women and children. As far as Hazel and I were concerned it was the same difference as steering a calf, and no bones were made of that, so why all the mystery? We concluded it was just one of those crazy ideas grownups have, and I guess that's all it was. The taboo was off when we were grown, and while it was a good deal bloodier operation on horses than it was on cattle, and made a colt awfully sick, and any brutality to horses was disgraceful, still it was just a castration, not a secret male rite of some kind. If one of the testicles was retained in the abdominal cavity and could not be removed, or for a few other reasons, the colt retained some of the characteristics of a stud, and he was said to be "cut proud."

There is a close empathy between men and horses. Horses, like men are prone to infection, and heal much more slowly than do cattle. One spring my children had pink-eye, and we left school until the malady was cured, going to the Roost, of course. The horses caught it, and we lost one mare that became blind and probably wandered off a ledge. The rest were pretty miserable until the epidemic subsided. Cattle had had pink-eye on the range for years, but neither the people nor the horses ever caught it from them.

While cattle were always branded when they changed hands, often horses were not; every horse was as well known as his owner throughout the country. Occasionally, though, it looked like a good idea to brand a young one that might stray away. My father didn't bother to throw one, he blindfolded the horse and branded him with a stamp iron, dabbing it on for only a second, as horses' skin is much finer than cows and his hair thinner. While the horse might flinch, he would be afraid to move if he couldn't see, and the branding was over so soon he didn't have time to put up a battle.

All of our life revolved around horses, and we enjoyed everything we did with or for them. Cowpunching was just plain hard work, but we did a lot of that, too.

9

Handling Cattle

WHEN WE WENT TO the Roost in 1909, Ern Wild, a childhood friend of my father's had his cattle there. He had said he was pulling out, it was too far from home. My father took care of Ern's cattle with his own the first winter, but when Ern came in the spring to make a deal to stay, Papa wouldn't deal. Ern said he had changed his mind and wanted to stay, but Papa said he only thought he had changed it, and offered to help him gather.

They were friendly enough, and rode and gathered Ern's few cows. Papa traded him a couple of cows for the C bull, giving him two of the old cows still trying to return to San Rafael. This was no problem to Ern, he planned to put them on Ferron Mountain in the summer and winter them at his ranch, thus giving them no opportunity to wander.

Every minute my father could spare from actually handling his cattle, was spent developing the range. He built corrals at the Roost, Twin Corrals, Hans Flat, The Gordons, Spur, some of them in the thick timber which he dragged into a circle and built into "brush" fences. But at the Roost and Crow Seep the corrals were stockade.

As soon as the ground thawed in the spring, a narrow trench was shoveled out. Short cedar and piñon posts were set in, fitted together so that their crooks made a smooth inside, and the dirt was tamped into the trench around them. A double strand of strong wire about halfway up further reinforced the fence, and after it had settled a year or two, it was there for the ages.

The corral at the Roost was one big round pen, but the one at the home ranch at Crow Seep was more complex. My father planned a smaller one on the north edge of the big main corral, with a holding pen and chute with squeeze gate between. Cattle turned from this squeeze could then be booted into either section. Cattle already in the corral could be crowded into the smaller square section, the gate closed and the main gate thrown open to receive another bunch.

From the gate west and south he built a wing a quarter of a mile or so. Cows came down this narrowing lane to the gate, hidden by the bulge of the corral fence so that they were practically into the enclosure before they began to find out what was up.

Our practice at the home ranch was to round up what cattle were out in the flats, drive them to the pond and pick up what was on water. Then we'd haze the whole bunch over the hill to the corral. The herd rolled over into the open place in front of the corral and the busy riders crowded the drags while the lead men kept the cattle from spilling around the point of the wing or around the body of the corral. In the resulting cloud of dust the cattle bellowed, the hoofs pounded, and each man gave a different yell, but no one stopped to listen.

If a cow broke back, a rider took after her and hazed her back into the bunch. If he needed help, another rider dropped in behind him. The trick was to head the cow, which would then make a quick switch and dart behind the rider, since she was smaller and quicker than the horse. That is where this following rider came in handy.

Not everyone knew this trick, and we often had visitors who tried to outrun both the rider and the cow, thus "laning" the animal and giving it no space to turn. This was looked down on as a "farmer" trick, but it did happen. In that case, if some visitor considered one of us girls, say, needed help and dashed out on the other side of the cow, he quickly found himself leading out, even at a disadvantage, while we backed him up About once and he got the message and tended to his own section of the herd from then on. After the cows were in the corral and the gate shut, everyone mounted up, and no matter how tired we were, ran a race to the saddle shed.

That first year, too, my dad saved his first bull at the Roost; he let a bull calf go uncastrated. In his herd was a big red, bald-faced cow, wide-hipped and rangey, but well filled in the back and loin, and with a gentle, intelligent head. Her bull calf, although brockle-faced, seemed to have a promising appearance, and we were setting standards. I have heard that Preston Nutter left every 10th bull calf uncastrated to furnish bulls for the future, but that is a tremendous number! Papa had always traded for or bought his bulls to bring new blood into his herd, Hereford if he could get it. He was breeding Hereford, but he was setting as the norm a big-boned, rangey type instead of the finely bred, small, blocky animal much in demand at the time. His bulls had to have long legs and be able to travel, they often ranged ten or more miles from water, going in to drink every other day or twice a week, and the water was often in deep canyons. Animals had to be built to cover ground.

With the C• bull he had five head, but his cows were scattered over a couple of hundred square miles of ridges, cedar breaks and prairies, and gathered only at the water holes.

Always in the summer he gathered and drove his cattle together, mixing them up, next year's calf crop uppermost in his mind, while he branded the current one.

One time we were camped on the point east of the Twin Corral reservoir when I was very small, probably the third or fourth summer at the Roost. We could hear a bull fight in progress, and rode down to watch C• and Thornton, a big red bull, fight it out. We stayed well back because these were big, heavy bulls, and when they "broke" from the head-lock, the breaking bull would rush blindly to escape the punishing horns of the victor. Both bulls would be massive destructive engines, and a rider caught by either or both in their line of blind flight would be gored and trampled into the ground. There was great danger, and we gave them a wide berth.

This was a bloody fight, and the combatants were so evenly matched that it lasted an hour or so before they both gave up, exhausted. I can't remember any more who was the winner, but I think it was the C• bull, and that Thornton was crippled for the rest of the summer.

I have seen bulls so gored in these fights that it is a wonder they could walk, and of course, they no longer had any value as sires. One bull returned by a man who had leased some cattle, was so crippled in one hind leg it could barely walk. This was in payment for a perfectly good bull, but the leaser was a good friend, so nothing was said about the deal; in fact, as I remember that deal, we were lucky to get *anything* back.

Bulls attained a definite status at the Roost, and considerable time was spent caring for them. In this high desert country, fall or winter calves either froze to death or lost ears or tail. The loss was too much to sustain, and early in his business, my father "managed" his calf crop by putting his bulls in a pasture about November and replacing them on the range, usually in a different location, the first of July.

Mama and Hazel and I questioned this date; it could have been a week or so later or earlier, but the first of July it remained. By the time the bulls were brought from Sams Mesa to the Twin Corrals and held all night, then cut out and scattered, it was too late to go anywhere to celebrate the 4th of July.

In later years there were two bulls for the Spur and two for the Gordons. These four were cut out of the herd first and two riders started out with them. When they got to the forks of the road above Hans Flat, they cut the bunch in two and one rider took the Spur bulls to the big tank in Spur Fork, and the other took his to French Seep. There were usually a few cows around the water, and after being sure the bulls had seen the water (they were more interested in the cows), we were free to jog back to camp at Twin Corrals.

Bulls for this middle of the range were cut out and left with whatever cattle were close by, and the ones for the Roost started down the draw with a couple of riders, and by late afternoon they were sipping from the troughs at the Roost Spring while they eyed the pickin's gathered all around— lonely heifers who had not seen them since the preceding fall.

Trailing bulls is altogether different from handling either stock cows or a herd of steers. You will have say, fifteen head moseying down the flat, and they travel *slow*. One of them finds a bone; he lets out a blurt, every bull comes to life. They gather round, giving vent to short, alarmed bellows, pawing dirt, running hither and thither in short bursts of speed, circling around the bone, smelling the ground, blowing blasts of air that kick up a real cloud of dust. All the while they are obviously in a state of mock terror. Cattle react to a carcass or to blood in this manner when driving a bunch of them along— but a *dry bone!* This sometimes ends in everyone settling down and meandering on down the trail as if nothing had happened, leaving the riders full of unanswered questions as to what it was all about, or it may end in several bull fights, all starting at once, some of them half-hearted sparring matches and one or two for real.

Remember how much muscle a bull carries in his massive neck and the size of his huge head and the needle sharpness of his horns. Hereford horns grew naturally with the tips pointed down, usually, but if the horn of a yearling looked like it was going to grow straight out or up, small weights with setscrews were attached to the tip of the horn. As the horn turned, sometimes these weights were changed for heavier ones, until about the age of two years, the horns were headed in the right direction. A standard head was about a quarter circle from the tip of one horn to the tip of the other—but, oh, that bone and meat behind it.

Fighting bulls meet head on, heads low, the horn bosses taking the pressure. The trick is to slide to the side, under the other bull's horn and gore shoulder or throat. But it seldom comes off that way, because the other bull is using the same tactics. Two bulls stand locked in combat, their front feet braced, their hind feet clawing for one more inch of purchase. Their necks swell, their sides heave, and every muscle in haunch and shoulder stands out like a rope. All the while, each head is moving ever so slightly, seeking that final thrust. Suddenly one bull weakens, turns to escape, a full three-quarters of a ton of beef at the speed of a locomotive, trampling everything in his path, slashing anything that comes in range of his swinging horns. The winner follows, no less blindly, trying to get close enough to bury a horn in any part of the fleeing loser. No rider *ever* gets close to fighting bulls, there is no way to tell which way they will break, or when.

While driving a bunch of cattle on the range, if bulls started fighting, we just drove the cows away from them and let them settle the matter. But on the way to the Roost with the bulls, we had to wait until the battle was over, then go on with the herd. Usually this didn't take long; the bulls had been together all winter and most of the contests had been settled.

My father thought the danger of bull battles would be minimized by polled bulls. These are naturally hornless. So he bought a bunch of them in later years. It's a cinch they didn't fight, or do anything else. Not being afraid of each other, they went to water in a bunch, shaded up in a bunch, grazed in a bunch, and were as exclusive as an old men's club. He spent the three or four years they were on the range dividing them up and driving them apart.

They were supposed to solve the dehorning problem, too, but they weren't so good at that, either. Feeders in the mid-west were demanding cattle that would crowd together without fear, feed at racks and water at troughs, and let a man walk among them without taking his life in his hands. Since these polled bulls didn't breed true, we were still faced with the painful job of dehorning the calves.

When branding, if there were two bulls in the corral that had been fighting, or if we thought they might, they were cut out as soon as the last cow went in the gate. It cost us calves the next year, perhaps, but it also saved having the corral torn down, or if it held, watching one very valuable animal kill another.

Range bulls were such fun; they took themselves so seriously. Down the trail to the waterhole, for the last mile or so, they "sang their way in." Heads lowered, eyes on the trail, swinging along rhythmically in a slow adagio, they murmured awful threats in a low, powerful *sotto voce* bellow. This would go on for a hundred yards or so, then up would come the big head and three or four blasts of such defiance would ring out, rising to a high-voiced shriek, that they left the animal himself somewhat startled. Sometimes he pawed deep gashes in the trail, throwing up scoops of dirt onto his powerful shoulders while he did some impromptu, off-the-script cursing.

Then he would lower his head again to swing back into his calypso of battles long won. My father could stand on a point above Twin Corral pond and hear three or four of his best bulls coming in down different trails, recognize them by their arias, and find life very sweet indeed.

We never fooled with a bull; if there was any risk the bull was cut out and hazed outside the corral. If a bull faced the branding fire and pawed dirt in warning, out he went with no delay. No one cornered a bull where he couldn't get away; if he wandered around the corral on the outside and got into the corner by the gate, he was booted out by the people in the corral before a rider came in to the gate. Bulls were a little wary of those hardtwist swinging men, too, so there wasn't the danger there is from a farm animal that knows no fear of man.

With the exception of branding we never, never, for any reason, handled our cattle afoot. In the first place, that is what we had horses for, and outside camp we were always mounted. Cows with little calves were untrustworthy for anyone afoot, and we treated them with necessary respect. Cows were cows, and they had their spheres of action; while we were not especially afraid of them, it was just the way the situation was, and we played it safe.

The one exception was branding, with the branding fire and calves between us and the cows. We would gather a bunch of cattle and take them to a corral. On the Gordons or the Spur, we included every cow we could find, but on Twin Corrals and the Roost we rode the range in geographical sections—Deadman one day, close around the Roost Spring the next, or maybe for a couple of days, Blue John one day and the Head of Antelope one day. Cows saw branded calves and tried to escape with theirs, so it took several roundups to get them all, and sometimes we didn't find one until the next spring.

After corraling, either the branding fire was kindled, or lunch was eaten if it was in order. We always had lunch at the Roost, partly because brandings were bigger there and the crew needed to be in good shape, and partly because Silver Tip Spring was close and we liked to picnic there.

Joe Biddlecome did everything in a workmanlike, efficient manner. He always used a running iron, long after these were illegal, because brands could be "drawn" instead of stamped. He found a copper head heated faster, burned clean after use, and made a clear, neat brand. He turned these irons out himself, making them a slender, wedge shape, about four or four-and-a-half inches long, three inches wide at the shoulder and tapered to two inches at the tip. The edges were a scant fourth of an inch thick, rounded and very smooth, with the corners rounded. The center of the iron was about $\frac{3}{8}$ inch thick, with two holes bored for the prongs of the handle, which was of scrap iron, to be riveted to it. The handles were some 24-30 inches long, with a looped end which served not only to carry the irons, usually four to eight in number, on a thong, but also to keep the iron from turning while in use.

To start a branding fire, we dug a shallow hole and buried a thick chunk of wood some three feet long, covering it well with dirt so it wouldn't burn out. Another chunk was placed about a foot or eighteen inches away from this and parallel, but it could burn, in fact it was meant to. Over these were laid the medium-sized side pieces and after the center was filled with tinder and chips and lighted, the top was covered with smaller wood. A good fire tender—and my mother was that—could make this fire last some three or four hours with minimal servicing.

Dirt was piled high against the outside buried chunk, some three or four inches higher than the wood and the irons were stuck in the fire, the copper heads six or eight inches into the center, and the handles parallel and covered well with dirt on the outside of this basic log. Theoretically, if the iron handle was kept well below the level of the head, and the dirt well heaped, it stayed a little cooler than the business end—but not much.

You'll never believe this, but cowpunchers did carry handkerchiefs, not for their usual use, but for branding-iron pads, and we used pieces of gunny sack and other padding also. If the iron handle proved a shade too warm, a front shirt tail was quick to get and of some help.

As soon as Hazel and I were big enough to swing a loop, nine or ten, we did the roping. Everyone helped and roping was easier than flanking or branding, beside being up out of the dust and heat. Mama tended the branding fire and vaccinated (for blackleg back in those simpler days!), and the alternate daughter helped flank and turn loose.

The hired man or men flanked and tied, as did Papa if he was not busy branding, marking, dehorning, etc., and when the operation swung into gear it was fast and fun. We were well aware that it was a painful operation for the calf, so we handled them as fast and carefully as possible.

Say it was Hazel's day to rope—sometimes we both roped, but that was not very satisfactory since we got in each other's way and the cattle were choused from both sides of the bunch, which crowded them unnecessarily. Out she comes with the first calf, bellering and bucking and hanging back on the rope.

As the calf reaches the proper place in the work arena, the flanker takes hold of the rope with his right hand and runs down it to the calf, which gives a big jump to escape. The flanker's right hand goes over the calf's nose as he grabs the knot of the rope under the calf's neck while he stretches over and catches the calf's left flank in his left hand. If this timing is good, the calf gives a big jump, and the flanker lifts and tips it over toward him. He falls with the animal, one knee landing in the calf's neck and the other in its flank with the four feet out in front of him. He quickly picks up the top front leg, bends it at the knee and holds it against the brisket while he gets his hogstring ready.

Sometimes I see a TV cowboy holding a calf with the leg straight out, and I shudder. With the leverage he could exert, this could well mean a broken or dislocated shoulder for the animal, but I never saw this injury on the range.

For some reason a slight twist to the leg will quiet a calf and make it quit kicking and wriggling. It may be painful, but if so, the calf doesn't indicate this by bellowing. I don't know what the reason is, it just works.

When I was small we used sash cord hogstrings with the loop about a third the way down on a nine- or ten-foot rope. The long end was threaded through the loop, and this running loop the flanker dropped over both front feet, shifting his right knee to the calf's ribs, and gathering in the flailing hind legs with his left boot until he could get the first wrap. He then gave all four legs a couple of turns, slipping the top hind foot down into place and tying above the ankles. Then he fished up the short end of the rope and tied a square knot. When my father did this himself, it was a work of art, but likely he changed to the end-looped hogstring because it was more secure.

After wrapping the legs of a calf with three or four turns of the end-looped hogstring, the flanker secured them with two half-hitches around the top front leg, either above the tie or around the foot. And he then went on to the next calf, which was bellering and hanging back on the end of Hazel's rope.

If we had enough help, sometimes we didn't tie, but held the calves. This took two men, the head man holding the bent front leg, with one of his knees in the calf's neck and the other wherever it was out of the way of the brander. The "heel" man held the hind legs, pushing the lower one up with his bootheel braced behind the hock joint so it couldn't get any purchase to kick or climb onto its feet. He straightened the top leg back; the trick was not to hold the calf from kicking by brute force, but to straighten the leg out and keep the calf from getting slack enough to kick. Both men turned the calf loose at the same time, the heel man rolling out of the way before the calf could kick him.

If the calf was close to the fire, Papa got his own iron, but if not, one of us brought him one. Mama often brought it when she came with the vaccine gun.

Don't ever believe that the proper temperature of the iron was cherry red—or white hot! That was too hot. It burned through the hide, making a brand that took too long to heal, and sometimes ended in a scaley white horny substances that could stand out as much as an inch or so from the hide as the animal got older. This could get knocked off by a tree limb or another animal, and leave a sore; although screw worms were not a problem this far north, it was poor herdsmanship. A "right" iron was one of that particular shade of light gray that copper takes just before it drops off into cherry red, and with all the hair from the previous use burned off cleanly.

With this unwieldly pencil my dad laid a brand on a wriggling calf as true as a die. In his early days he branded JOE which he called Hip-Side-and-Shoulder, on the left side. But when he settled at the Roost, it was no longer necessary to use such a big brand, and he used diamonds. He liked diamonds, they went on easy, looked good, were too big to skin out and work over, and they identified his outfit. Not matter how far a cow strayed, if she carried some kind of diamond, anyone seeing her knew her for ours.

His first diamond brand was Meathooks ⬦ a really beautiful brand, but because of the curves, he had to abandon it when he was no longer doing all the branding. He used the

Diamond-and-a-Half ✩ for a while, then the Bar-Diamond-Slash, and finally the Diamond Slash, ◇\ . He finally settled on the Diamond-and-a-Half, which he sent in to be recorded. This is a common brand, and was already on the books, so he was awarded the ✩ , still a Diamond-and-a-Half according to the bureaucratic lights of the brand recorder, but of some irritation to Papa because he didn't so consider it.

As the calf branding got to be a bigger project, and he had more help, he delegated the branding, but he always did the knife work himself. In later years, when I was running the outfit, I found I had to do that, too. Steers were our product, and in those years the market was slow and reluctant —any non-uniformity was subject to cut in price. He didn't want his steers yanked down in the back by pulling the cords out entirely, nor the calf subjected to unnecessary surgery if one of the testicles was allowed to slip back up into the body after the bag was cut off. Nor did he want the animal to bleed too much from faulty knife work, so he did the castrating and scraped the cords to suit himself.

Other than brands there were also earmarks. A swallow-fork was made by creasing the ear lengthwise and cutting a sloping notch out of the tip. An under-half (under-half-crop, but the "crop" was not usually stated) was made by slitting the ear and cutting the lower half straight across about a fourth or a third of the way down. There were other marks, like cutting the top cord of the ear and making it droop, or cropping it off, but we considered these disfigurements.

In his never-ceasing desire to make cowpunching at least comprehensible to his wife, my father early used waddles on the jaws of the heifers as a further identification. A waddle is made by cutting a flap of skin; when it heals, it pulls around into a roll, and if cut slim at the top, dangles. It can be anywhere on a cow, but is usually around the head or neck;

and makes a fine identification during the winter when brands
are haired over. Waddles—any knifework!—are slower heal-
ing than the brand.

That flap of skin from a cow's throat to her brisket has
been carved into more dewlaps, jughandles, bells and such
than man can even remember. Cut up close to the head so it
hangs from the throat, it is called a bell waddle, and is a
distinctive, pretty mark but a damn nuisance if there is ever
occasion to rope a cow. It almost always gets jerked off.

My father used jaw waddles, and he cut them himself,
by lifting a flap of skin on the calf's top (left) jaw and running
his knife blade through, pulling it some three inches toward
the eye and then out, leaving a flap. The right waddle was
cut by turning the head up, which made it run toward the ear.
When healed, the right hung just a shade lower, but when he
rode up to a bunch of cows and they raised their heads to look
at him, their white faces squared by those ornamental waddles,
they looked good to him.

We girls started our herds early, but what was Papa's
he considered "Tootsie's" also, and not for years and years did
she have a separate brand.

My herd developed from the Picert Cow. Ollie Picert
stole a little red heifer calf from someone and "sleepered" it,
gave it an insignificant earmark he could either claim or not as
discretion directed. My father's riding was not exclusively
confined to the Roost; he rode the outside ranges "to keep his
neighbors honest" and just to look around. He often had a few
calves at the place in Hanksville, and sometimes turned them
out on the range there for a time, and his cows often strayed
from the Roost to the Dirty Devil River. He got onto this
red calf deal some way, and it was too good to pass up.

He roped and branded the little red heifer, but since the
calf was becoming too well known, and he wasn't trying to
"break into the pen" (penitentiary), he maverick branded the

calf with a Flying Diamond $-\diamondsuit$. This was before the diamond became almost his trademark, so he could renounce the brand if Picert got nasty.

Picert, although hot under the collar, didn't have the guts to claim the calf, and Papa drove it to Hanksville, then to the Roost, and from it sprang a considerable herd for me. And I kept the brand.

At first Hazel also branded Flying Diamond on the ribs (mine was over the hip bone), but this left us without a distinguishing mark for our personal things, so she changed hers to Bar Diamond $\lozenge\!\!\backslash$, which she ran from about 1915 until her death in 1969.

If we needed to rope and throw a grown cow, which we called "big stuff," we handled her differently from calves. Someone roped a cow's head and another roper, usually my father since he was the best roper I ever saw, picked up her heels, cutting her from the bunch and hazing her near the fire while he caught her. Between the two ropers, they stretched the cow out on her belly, and someone grabbed the tail and yanked her over on her side. Then the tail was brought up through between her hind legs and past her flank, and a man reared back on it.

One man can hold down a grown cow with this hold, since cattle get up hind quarters first. If she is thin, this is easy; if she is fat, there doesn't seem to be enough tail. Here again, great caution and skillful knee pressure is required to keep her hips pinned to the ground, and yet not roll the animal over to squash the holder; also, she can deliver a stunning whack with her flailing head.

The ropes are then put on the feet, no point in choking a cow to death just to vent a brand or saw off a stub horn! The holding horses are brought up close and the ropes tied short, keeping the feet raised high.

When ready to turn loose, both men mount up and untie

the dallies from the saddle horns and throw down plenty of slack. She kicks around getting to her feet and opens up the loops so the ropes fall off. A stupid horseman who doesn't pay out enough rope so that the cow can kick it off, causing the loop to draw up on one foot, is much cursed; it takes a lot of flipping to dislodge the drawn-up loop, and make it slide down over the ankle.

If it was necessary to mark a cow temporarily, her tail was "bushed," the tassle cut off square. This lasted for several months, and anyone seeing it, would tell us about seeing her.

After being thrown and worked on, a cow always gets up "on the prod," and chases the innocent bystander up a fence every time. She doesn't tackle the horsemen, although they arm themselves with a double hardtwist just in case. It doesn't pay to stand around and gawk when a cow finds she is free.

Once in a while during calf branding, a cow found her calf and followed it in to the fire. Usually she was scared, anyway, and the rider could boo her back into the bunch. But, if he wasn't handy, the flanker kicked her face full of dust, which by this time was ankle deep, and she turned back into the sheltering herd, blinded for a few minutes. If she was coming in too fast and fighty, she got slapped across the nose with a Stetson in addition to the dust treatment, and I never saw one that needed more than that. Cows mostly bluff, and a person can stand his ground, yell and wave his arms so they often swerve aside at the last minute.

During branding there was so much confusion in the bunch that a cow rarely found her calf. The full symphony of the branding corral included her constant calling, the answering brass yammering of the unbranded calves for their mothers, the staccato "brt" of the calf suddenly discovering he is caught by the roper, the counterpoint bellering of the calf coming in to the fire, as he bucks and bawls, the overtone wails of the calf being branded, all underlain by the percussion of trampling hoofs, cymbal clink of spurs and bridles, sharp crack of ropes, bass grunts of flanked calves and perhaps a short arpeggio of excited laughter now and then.

There is no other activity in the world to equal the branding corral's excitement and involvement; it is not a one-dimensional symphony of sound, but of all the senses. There is no other smell so rich as that of dust, burned hair (but different —this has such a clean, wholesome odor!), horse sweat, aromatic piñon smoke from the fire and the sweet smell of cattle. Our eyes smarting with sweat and dust eagerly scan the color and movement. Hereford cattle are so beautiful with their white faces and glowing red bodies. The swing and precision movements of roper and horse, acting as one are miracles of grace. The feel of the ropes, of the clean, warm, silky calves, of the tools of our trade—the living chain of sight, smell, taste, touch blends into my mind as I look back, filling my memory with glory and my homesick heart with balm.

Hazel and me tying down a calf. My father is just coming into the picture, and we welcome his help.

Mama and Papa. She is wearing a horsehair hatband.

10

Wildlife—Primary and Secondary

WHEN WE MOVED to the Roost there were great herds of antelope around North Springs and in the head of Antelope Valley; in fact, all over the San Rafael Desert. They didn't range much beyond the Roost Spring, as they preferred the sand grass (Indian Rice Grass) and oak browse areas. When the summer rains brought out the sunflowers and other lush weeds, they held mostly in the blow-sand dunes, where the grazing was better. They usually did not go to water, although I have seen herds coming back from watering at the Roost, and in later years we found their tracks at the pond at Crow Seep.

Antelope are most interesting; they are curious and friendly and they play regular games of their own. One game is outrunning anything and dashing in front of it. This was fun when the roads were first put into the Roost and cars could travel a little faster than horses. The antelope herd would swoop down from a sidehill, or up from a swale, run alongside the road and finally, after a real burst of speed, cross in front of our vehicle. It was a game with us, too, and we speeded up as much as we dared in the more or less parallel cow trails which served for roads, and made them really lay to the ground to outrun us. It cost us springs, but it was worth it!

Antelope tracks are similar to deer tracks, but are more delicate and the toes are more slim and pointed. Along the rims of the sand dunes their tracks lay like lace edges, and as they didn't go to water and were not "trailing" animals, but grazed individually, this lace was wide and intricate.

We thought they marked out boundaries to their territories, too. As they crossed a trail, they pawed out a slight depression, the long, fine scratches running out sometimes as much as two or three feet from the center of the "hole" into which they planted their sign, a pile of manure.

They shared our hatred of rattlesnakes, too. Often we would find where they had killed a snake in a space about six or eight feet square. This was usually on a trail, since the snakes seemed to like to travel in the soft trails, but we did find the marks of the battle in the sandbumps, too. Apparently, wherever an antelope buck ran onto a rattlesnake, that snake was immediately stamped not only to death, but also into minute pieces.

An antelope kid could keep up with its mother when it was no more than a couple of days old, but was easy prey to coyote or eagle before it could travel. However, whether large antelope were pulled down during the winter time by pack-running coyotes, I don't remember, but it is likely they were, especially sick or old ones.

While there were a few deer on North Point when I was young, now there are deer other places on the Roost as well, but so few that there is no point hunting them. It is not deer range, really, as there isn't enough browse to support these brush eaters.

Porcupines lived in the piñon trees, and some of the marks where they had eaten the bark from high limbs were years and years old. They are much more numerous now than they used to be; it was quite a treat to run onto their tracks when I was a youngster, with the brush marks of their swishing tails overlying the deeply dented tracks that looked like they had been printed by tiny human feet.

Besides the rattlesnakes, there were bull snakes (we called them blow snakes), racers and a very few watersnakes usually along the rivers or in deep, wet canyons.

Several kinds of lizards were common, from the big blue-throated tree lizards found usually around cottonwood trees, to the slick-looking whip lizards which I remember most around the Roost Spring. The little rock lizards were everywhere. Driving the steers to town across the San Rafael desert during the breeding season of the desert lizards, found them covered with brilliant red and yellow spots, and also found them willing to fight the tempting dangling end of a lasso, especially after the many trampling feet of the steer herd had stirred them up.

Among the birds I especially remember the crows, piñon jays and cowbirds. An eagle, either bald or golden, stayed around sometimes, and hawks were common. Nighthawks trilled their plaintive night calls, and we kids enjoyed their nests, just a dent under a log where the mother bird looked exactly like a weathered pine knot until we stirred her up and made her fly off the two white eggs. She would then limp off, dragging a wing, looking like a badly wounded bird, but after she had tolled us away from the nest, she would fly away.

Mourning doves were everywhere, and they nested only on the ground, scraping together a few twigs to hold their eggs from rolling away. These eggs were incubated mostly by the hot desert sun.

The cowbirds nested in bushes, and in the spring we often saw a bird dart out and we rode over to look down and find the hidden nest with its four or five speckled eggs.

We found a hawk's nest once, on the ridge of the Long

Draw of Roost Flats. We played with the little white hawks for a few days, riding the five or six miles for the privilege. We didn't kill them; we didn't kill anything but rattlesnakes, but we enjoyed playing with the baby hawks.

We often caught baby cottontails and cuddled them in our hands for a few minutes, then turned them loose and went back to cowpunching.

Although there must have been dozens of kinds of rodents and small moles and such that we never happened to see— a desert teems with life—we were fond of and pestered by three varieties of rodents: the striped ground squirrels, the little red chipmunks and the kangaroo rats.

The kangaroo rats came out only at night, where they hop-hopped around, stuffing anything they could find in the way of food into their cheek pouches, hopping back to their burrows. They were rather pretty, gray on the back, but white underneath with their strong, heavy tails, white bushed. In a night they could carry off a sack of oats, much needed by our saddle horses, if we didn't put a stop to their depredations by covering the grain tightly.

The chipmunks and ground squirrels were cute, but they ate into the grain supply pretty badly, too, stuffing their cheek pouches until they were nearly too top heavy to travel. But they buried their "loot." In the spring tufts of oats came up all over the place, but I never could see the straight-line pattern that legend credited them with using so that they could come back and find their caches. I never noticed many places where they had dug up their stores, either. After a good piñon-nut crop, tiny clumps of piñon sprouts were everywhere.

Some of the ranches poisoned these pests, but they died all over the place, making such a mess that we didn't bother with that. We kept cats at the cabin at Crow Seep.

We had a lot of trouble keeping a cat at the Roost, holding the supply to one or two tom cats since we didn't plan to populate the countryside with them. The supply of chipmunks would just about support a couple of cats year round when we weren't there to feed them, although Blue and Whiteman, big emasculated toms, often caught half-grown rabbits.

Sometimes cats would start to eat lizards in the summer, probably because these were easy to catch. But they had a kind of poison that would all but kill a cat. By fall, he would be so thin he could hardly walk, with his hair rough, his eyes looking three times as big as natural in his boney head. During the winter when he couldn't get the lizards that he seemed to crave, he would get fat and sleek, but he would do the same thing over the next season.

Coyotes were not much of a threat to our house cats, but for some reason bobcats will kill every housecat they get a chance at. Finally my father cut a hole in the cabin door just big enough for the house cat to get through, and when a bobcat chased him into the cabin when we weren't there, he was safe. We often found tracks of where the bobcat had prowled around the cabin, looking into this hole which was too small for him.

Bobcats put us out of the chicken business from time to time, too. They couldn't get into the coop, but all they had to do was wait until morning and out would come a hen for feed or water (we taught them to water at the pond, but we left feeders full of grain for them), and then nail her. This must have been a great treat; a fat hen was much bigger than a skinny jack rabbit, and much easier to catch.

Rabbits there were by the million, almost; both jack rabbits and cottontails. They, together with the rodents, furnished food for coyotes, foxes, both red and gray, and for the bobcats. Coyotes were plentiful, and a real menace to the calves for many years until "1080" and cyanide guns thinned them almost to the vanishing point. The biggest mistake of this campaign was the killing of the foxes, which allowed the seedeating rodents to overrun and almost denude the ranges. Foxes didn't bother calves, but this was not true of their bigger cousins, the coyotes.

Coyotes ate a lot of calves for us during our first years at the Roost, and left a lot more bobtailed. Now and then a calf would survive with a bite taken out of the ham. Coyotes are like wolves, they eat the animal while it is still living, and they were sometimes scared off before they got the calf killed. One little cow, after losing the top out of one hind leg when she was a calf, grew up so warped and crippled that she could hardly make it to water and back as a result of this voracious savagery.

All of the animals native to the country were primary wildlife, but when cattle and horses ran loose on the range, subject to all the weather conditions and to the dangers from predators, they were no longer domesticated livestock, but became *secondary* wildlife. Cattle drifted back into the heavy timber and eluded the riders, sometimes for years. At the Roost this rough country was limited, and with few exceptions, we gathered the cedar cattle and corralled and handled them. This took considerable skill; these cattle were "snuffy" and most reluctant to be put into a bunch of gentle cattle. They kept trying to break out, but we watched and were right there when one stuck his frowny head out of the main herd. After a while they would usually settle down and not give us any trouble until the next roundup.

My father could run his eye over a dayherd and tell by the well-smeared hind quarters of a few of them which cows had put up the hardest runs. A scared, running cow squirts quantities of partially digested manure, some of which she smears around her hips with her switching tail. The spattered tracks of running cattle gave rise to an expression used commonly, "Gave me a slick trail to run on." This meant that the pursuit was fast and close.

Eweneck was one of these wild ones. She was around for several years; I note in my mother's diaries that she was mentioned in 1921, and we sold her—much subdued, and I thought it was a shame!—in about 1936. She ran on North Point, out from Frenchy, in country rather limited so that it didn't pay to ride it often.

She was called Eweneck because that described her. She was always skinny, high-wethered, rack-hipped and slab-sided, her ugly old head carried on a skimpy neck that sagged like an old ewe's. While descriptive, the name also expressed a cowman's amused contempt of her, which bothered her little, apparently.

Eweneck always had a calf, and we always branded it as a yearling, roping and leading it in. We didn't try to drive her into the bunch; after all, she was colorful and we let her enjoy her freedom.

One spring Mama jumped Eweneck and her big calf. They tore off into the cedars, with Mama doing all right, running right up on the old cow. Eweneck's yearling dropped under a sheltering cedar—and Mama saw him. That was about the end! If she had run Eweneck's calf to death instead of roping him (which she couldn't have done in any event) there would be hell to pay. Pulling her horse in, she went back to see what the damage was, and as she rode within ten or twelve feet of the yearling, lying close to the tree trunk with its eyes tightly shut, it opened them and darted out from under close limbs. Like a fawn, it had hidden from the rider.

Calves were born in the spring during the whelping season of coyotes, which brought about heavy losses. The mother coyote had neither the time nor the strength to run down more elusive prey, so she hid and watched. A lone cow would hide her calf and hurry to water and back. By the time he was a couple of weeks old he could make the trip of seven or eight miles to water, but those first few critical days, she had to leave him under a bush. He was taught to remain there, and no fawn ever lay any tighter to cover. However, he lacked the fawn's protection of non-scent, and he was smelled out from time to time. If not rescued, he then made a meal, or several of them, for a ravenous mother coyote.

While these calves lay close and hidden from a rider, a herd of cattle going past would often bring them out. If we drove cows down a flat or a ridge where there were little white-faced calves under brushes, and they came and joined the herd, we left them strictly alone. When they didn't find their mothers, they returned to the bush and lay down again. If they were scared by our trying to cut them back or otherwise handle them, they forgot where they had been left and the returning cows couldn't find them. A cow would bawl around a day or two, but when her overfull udder quit hurting, she gave him up and quit hunting him. The calf would then be a dogey, and probably wind up piece by piece in some coyote den.

A social development came about when the cattle became more numerous on the range, a cow "kindergarten" system. This was a group of little calves under the protection of one or two mothers. As many as twelve or fifteen cows and their calves would band together and the calves never be left without a couple of nurse cows near them. I have even seen yearling heifers standing guard over three or four calves. This is common on any range, and betokens more communication and social mores than animals are usually given credit for.

Horses, too, lived under secondary wildlife conditions, but they were different. Not being subject to many predators, they faced other problems of survival. They were more intelligent than cows and their social rules were more complex and closer to the primary way of life.

The few horses at the Roost were dropouts from Butch Cassidy's Wild Bunch, or from J. B. Buhr's fine stock, but those on San Rafael Desert were from further back. They had been there fifty years or more before we went to the Roost; they were inbred, with the only size given to them by Percheron forebearers, which added little to their value as saddle stock.

Along about 1904 or 1905, Swaseys and some others had taken a bunch of mares into the Roost to try to raise mules. Ern Wild was interested in this venture, too. My mother quotes it in her poem about the Roost, but I can remember stories of their mismanagement, the worst of which was to put their mares on Sams Mesa for the winter. Sams Mesa is loco country, and this was a late wet spring; the loco grew like a field of alfalfa. All of the mares succumbed to it, and when the boys went back in about June, the few live ones were skeletons, nothing but skin and bone, and with not enough coordination remaining to get them down and back to the deep canyon spring for water. The boys shot the remnant and called the project a failure.

On the desert Swaseys had also put some good horses, and the whites and grays of her descendants of these horses showed considerable breeding. Somewhere there had been a strain of Appaloosa; white hipped colts were still showing up in the last remnants of the San Rafael Desert wild horses in the 1940s. The big bands were gone by then, and with horse roundups aided by airplanes the last few have finally been gathered. I never thought to see the time that I could stand on Lookout Point at Keg and not see a horse—I have seen as high as ten or twelve big bands from that vantage point, with a few scattered colts here and there.

When my youngest son, Noel, learned to fly in the early 1950s, he had his own plane, an Aeronca, and his pal, Bobby Tidwell, Leland's son, flew the club Cub from Green River. They flew sorties all over the country and had a ball. At that time there were still small bands of wild horses, and the boys found it was great fun to buzz a bunch and watch them lay to the ground and run. When Noel told me, I replied with the story that was told when I was their age, about Bobby's grandfather, Frank Tidwell.

It was said that a fellow was touring Hell one time, with the Devil for his guide. Going from one place to another, they passed a huge iron kettle turned upside down, and this visitor saw some human fingers clawing out from under the edge of this kettle. He ran to turn it over and liberate the poor wretch.

"Hold on!" said the Devil. "Don't do that! That's Frank Tidwell under there, and if you turn him loose, he will have Hell full of wild horses before morning!"

A desert stud was about the toughest animal alive; he had to be to get to the position of leader and hold it. His bunch of mares, some fifteen or twenty head, was his harem, and their welfare was his first concern.

While they grazed in the lush, grassy valleys, he stood on a high point and looked around. If he was satisfied that nothing threatened them, he grazed, too, but always on the outer fringes of the herd. And he kept his eye on the mares so that they didn't stray away.

When it was time to go for a drink, if there hadn't been rain or snow to put water in the shallow depressions of the flat slickrock, he rounded up his bunch and put them on the trail toward Dugout, Cottonwood, Tanks of the Desert, Keg or the San Rafael watering places. Always there was an old, wise mare that led out; she was his second in command, and while she didn't chastise the wrongdoers like he did, still, in the social structure she was the first and no other mare ever challenged her position.

Horses were "trailing" animals. They lined out behind a leader, often in single file, and they traveled at a good fast trot. The stud brought up the rear, the vulnerable position, for that is where men were likely to appear.

When the bunch got close to water, on the lip of Keg

Canyon, say, the stud rounded them close and left them standing in a tight bunch, ready to run at his slightest command. He dropped over the rim, down the trail, smelling the tracks for the familiar hated smell of iron, the bushes on each side of the trail for the man smell, and he watched all the rims. Only the extreme need for water forced him into this dangerous position, so easy for man to make into a deadly trap.

Arriving at the water, he drank sparingly, snorting and watching. If nothing stirred, if he decided it was worth the risk to bring in the mares, he raced nervously back and started them down the trail, watching the back trail with great trepidation. The mares didn't waste any time, either, going down to the spring, drinking and coming right back out.

The stud had watched everything, and when the lead mare topped out, he rounded the bunch again, starting them up the trail, while he dropped back into the canyon to drink his fill. When he came out, the mares were still trotting up the valley behind the old leader, colts running close alongside their mothers. He overtook them and put them back on the grazing range.

Studs had their territory, marked on the boundaries and on the high lookout points by piles of manure, which were added to every time the owner passed. We called these stud piles (when my mother wasn't around to hear us!) and sometimes they would be two or three feet high, hold ten or twelve bushels of manure above ground, and who knows how much the sand had covered over the years these had served as boundary markers.

Bands of wild horses rarely met accidentally, every stud knew where all the other horses in the country were, and he didn't plan to run into another leader, which would mean a battle. In the spring, life took on a little zing and they all tossed caution overboard in the interest of conquest. An experienced old leader often added two or three mares to his harem by taking them away from a younger stud, usually a four or five-year-old just beginning to herd. This was relatively easy, and although the younger horse fought valiantly, he was no match for the old veteran, and went off over the hill ahead of the winner, losing strips of hide and hair every time the old horse could get close enough. This taught him a lesson—that here was no sparring match like he had fought with his peers in the past spring seasons.

Sometimes bands did run together going to or coming from the few watering places. In that case, there was a set of rules as exact as any that men have formed for conquest. The mares were convivial and wanted to mix, but they were put in their places as soon as the first stud saw what had happened and dropped down off his high lookout to straighten things out. By that time the other stud was also pounding in and things had gone far beyond a peaceable settlement. Both leaders were whipping their mares back into two bunches with an arena between them. Woe to the ignorant or unwary mare that stepped out of line for a bite of grass or to smell noses with an opposing mare. The fight was suspended until her leader showed her where she belonged.

The two studs approached each other on tiptoe and warily. Smelling noses, nostril to nostril, not tip to tip, suddenly they reared, their long yellow teeth bared for whatever part of the adversary that could be fastened to, and their flinty hoofs striking and raising bumps on the head and shoulders of the foe. They fell back, each trying to bite the throat out of the other, while protecting his own. It is said that wild jackasses could kill a stud at just this point, by tearing out his throat. Two horses would rarely kill each other, but they might tear out big strips of skin, knock off hair and hide from each other's heads and when they whirled and kicked after coming to the ground, sometimes broke legs or caved in ribs. It was a rare old stud that didn't bear awful scars of past fights.

The battle would be waged back and forth between the lines of the mares for upwards of half an hour or more. From the first whuffle! as they smelled nostrils, there was a constant screaming of defiance and pain from both horses. It would be noisy and exciting exhibition, and clouds of dust were stirred up.

Finally both horses would be foaming, with sweat and blood streaming, and their raucous breathing might be heard for a mile. The battle would end suddenly, with one horse leaving the arena as fast as he could make it, the victor in the same depleted condition hastening his departure with tooth and hoof, deftly dodging the answering kicks of the vanquished.

The victor then would look the new mares over while he regained his wind, and put them into his bunch, showing them who was boss with ruthless force, and the bunches mingled and traveled out to feed or in to water.

For a few days the old stud would be sore and stiff, and the lead mare did most of the decision making as to where they should graze or travel, while a new pecking order was evolved. His disposition was not very kindly, and if necessary he could enforce his authority on some young, headstrong mare.

I have heard my dad say that in running wild horses in the spring when the mares were heavy with foal, if one became winded and could no longer keep up with the rest, she would turn and run in the opposite direction just as fast as she could. If the stud, racing around the herd frantically, should happen to see her in time, he would chastise her soundly and put her back into the horse herd.

When a mare foaled, particularly the older ones, she pulled off to herself, and if the stud found her, he let her alone, but watched carefully until she was ready to rejoin the herd in some 24 hours. However, he might forget one, and these stray mares were found by the young studs to start their herds.

When the horse colts were yearlings, the stud whipped them out, but not very forcefully until they were twos. That spring he would not tolerate them anywhere near the bunch, and most bands had a small clot of these twos and threes following along. Of course the mare colts were kept, it was the males that might threaten his reign. It was these young horses that the horse-chasers were after, not the mares and certainly not the old stud, who would be far too set in his ways to break to ride.

My mother tells about one horse chase she was on when one of the fellows roped an old stud and tied him to the wagon wheel, there not being any trees on the desert. The old horse had fought the men by every means in his power, but they choked him down and put a hackamore on him, dragged him up to the wheel to tie him. He stood there that night, but the next day he threw himself on the ground and died before night.

He tried to kill every man who came near him, and when he was down and almost dead, my mother's skirt came almost within striking distance as she walked past on her regular camp duties, and he grabbed at that, his ugly yellow teeth clicking like a bear trap. When he was dead, wherever man had touched him there was a swelling, his hate had been that virulent.

Studs were in their prime from about six or seven to about fifteen years of age, when some younger horse would finally whip him and take his mares. These old renegades followed the bands, probably finally fighting so desperately that they died from the wounds received, or they winter killed, partly because they had lost heart.

The mares might have had a life span a few years longer, but not much—winters were hard, the restrictions of living in a tight bunch depleted the grazing rapidly and the mares were not always in the best physical condition, after raising a colt going into winter thin and weak.

It was a tough life, complicated by harrassment by men, the only predator the horse had. On the open range he was as much a native as an antelope, but not quite the same—he was *secondary* wildlife.

Roy Dickerson

In the spring we gathered the yearling steers and put them into Horseshoe Canyon. When we were ready to trail them to Green River to the railroad, the latter part of May, we collected them and drove them up the Sandslide out of the canyon. This is the herd in the canyon.

11

Hired Men and Visitors

REMEMBER THAT WE felt we were
the ruling family; if people didn't like the way we did things,
they could go somewhere else, but if they stayed with us, they
did it our way. And while our rules of conduct were few, they
were strict. As long as we didn't interfere with each other,
and did our share of the work, we had almost complete
personal freedom. This developed us into rank individualists,
and the visitors who most enjoyed staying at the Roost were
the ones of the same stamp of character.

In telling of these people who meant the most to us,
I might step on some toes; if so, remember that some of the
stories I hear of my childhood make me see red. Only lately
I was much offended by one that included our cursing each
other. There was not a word of truth in it, it was a total
misrepresentation and very unfair, but since we did use pro-
fanity constantly and casually, the poor man thought he was
telling the truth. He just didn't know the rules, one of the
strictest of which and the most likely to bring down the punishing wrath of our elders, was to use even one swear word to or
about another person—it simply wasn't tolerated.

I tell this to point up the fact that in all probability some of the people in this chapter will not agree with my delineation of their characters, and they do have my sympathy. Not only that, I'll paraphrase Marie Antoinette and say, "let 'em play their tune." And the smallest violins make the sweetest sounds.

The Roost was isolated, and visitors were more than welcome. In frontier fashion they often stayed a week— a month. Some of them were still there for the next branding-steer-fall ride and became a part of our lives.*

Two of these men grew so dear to us and were so much a part of the outfit, that it would be unfair not to tell about them. One was Hans Andersen, who must have worked for us a couple of years or more when we girls were little, and Roy Dickerson (Little Dick) who worked off and on for several years during my teens.

Hans Andersen was a small, red-headed Irishman, droll and sweet-tempered. He loved us little girls well, and we returned his affection whole-heartedly. He was considerate and kind to Mama and she liked him, too. He was a good stockhand, tended to business and was completely reliable, so was a top hand as far as my father was concerned.

Hans left his mark on the range in Hans Flat (we were still naming the range) at the head of the Spur. We camped there one summer, the summer of the yellow-jackets, and he was always comforting when we appealed to him. He "played the spoons" which has become popular on Lawrence Welk's show, but his "spoons" were often two sections of cow ribs. They made a rhythmic rattle accompaniment to his whistled or hummed tunes.

---

*When Arthur and Hazel were married, they started a ranch across the Green River, in the Big Flats and Doobinkey area near the present Dead Horse Point. In hiring a man strange to the country and its customs, Hazel told him, "You know we are a long way from town and dependent on each other for companionship. Therefore, we will treat you as a member of the family—" after a thoughtful pause—"God help you!"

After he left the Roost, Hans drifted up into the northern part of the state, where he became a wheat rancher and married and raised a fine family. I met his wife and children in the 1950s when I worked (until I was fired for writing the editor a poem!) for the Tremonton *Leader* newspaper. The Andersens lived there and from my remembered affection, I looked them up and was often a guest in their home.

Once I was sitting at the kitchen table drinking coffee while Hans and Irene were doing the dishes. She had just been fitted with her first hearing aid, and was telling how wonderful it was to be able to hear again. She had become progressively deaf since girlhood, and had gone to church for years, sitting quietly in the congregation without hearing one word that was spoken. She was delighted to be a real part of the meeting and thrilled to hear her family, too.

"Why, I don't know how Hans ever put up with my failing all these years," she chatted affectionately.

Hans stood drying a plate, and he paused while he looked back in memory, then turned to her and said in surprise, "Why, I never even noticed it." He was so honest that she couldn't help but believe him, and so did I. And I thought, how characteristic of the kind Hans!

After the summer at Hans Flat, we camped the next year south of the spring at Crow Seep, and I am sure that Hans helped scrape out the first sand from the pond. He cheerfully did whatever there was to be done.

Another memory of Hans, or connected with him, that comes to mind was Hazel's doll. In those days the dolls were made with cloth-and-sawdust bodies and bisque heads, which were not water resistant. This doll which Hazel had lovingly named Hans, was left out in the rain, and the head weathered into a crackled finish, some of the flakes chipping off until he was pretty tacky looking.

We were camped on the Head of the Spur, where Papa

had been putting in a trough at Burro Seep, named that because the first time he rode into the canyon, a big, black burro was pawing out a hole to get a drink. He had no special time to do maintenance work, whenever he got around to something, he did it. He had been hauling the red paint for the wagon, and one afternoon, he got a couple of hours and did the job.

Hazel and I played house close by, and during the painting project Hazel wandered over, Hans cuddled in her arms. She and Papa started visiting, and he remarked on Hans' decrepit appearance. They decided to improve the doll with a coat of wagon paint. This didn't seem odd to us little girls; as soon as the paint was dry, we treated him the same as always, loving him even more dearly. His appearance startled visitors, though.

Little Dick was a small, gnarled, dark-complexioned fellow, with light gray eyes, almost buried in the sun- and laugh-wrinkles of his· face. The first time he came to the Roost, he was headed for the Arizona Strip with a small band of horses. The Roost is not directly on the line of travel from southwestern Colorado where he had grown up, to the Arizona Strip, but he had been raised on legends of "Rimrocker Pete" as my father had been known in western Colorado in his youth, and Dick planned to stop off and see if those legends of that long loop and general cow competence were justified. I believe he always thought they were, he admired and respected my Dad greatly. We learned some years later that he had been also a matrimonial truant, if not a downright fugitive.

Little Dick was fully as much of an individualist as any of us, and he left his mark on the family and the outfit. He held a low opinion of women and children in general, maintaining that most "dry nester families" as he characterized any family living on any ranch, did nothing but mess in the yard and burn up boards. Lumber was always scarce and valuable, but easy to chop into firewood, and as I have picked my way gingerly across the dooryard to the outhouse on several ranches, I agreed with him. He didn't cherish that opinion of us; he thought we might be worth saving since we girls were in St. Marys-of-the-Wasatch most of the year, and he could endure us over the summer.

The one thing we did that nearly drove him crazy was the way we scattered the camp around—"like them Chaffins" as he put it. Particularly hobbles. When we camped away from the home ranch we kept a cavvy of some twenty or thirty horses, since we each required a string of four or five and there were always a few colts being broken or other excess. All these had to be hobbled every night, and the hobbles taken off to drive the horses to water or into camp every morning. Dick was usually the wrangler when he was around, and he got up early to get the horses before they shaded up and were impossible to see among the trees.

When Dick first came to work for us we were using strap hobbles, mostly, the supply eked out by raveling one-inch soft-twist rope twisted between the horse's legs and "buttoned" around the knot in the end. These were theoretically taken off and put around a horse's neck when he was turned loose, but after Dick had been with us a while, they were mostly carried in by the jingler.

Dick opined we tossed them in the hardest places to find as we brought them in. In desperation about our casualness about this, he laid out a hobble sack, and woe to the person who neglected to put the extra hobbles in it. Since this was in the interest of conserving equipment and of keeping the camp more ship-shape, my father backed him up. The Chaffin boys and the Tidwells were spending considerable time with us about then, so he usually had someone on the grill about it every day or two.

Horses at the Roost were never again the same after Dick started working for us. We had usually handled our horses quite openly, and if we couldn't catch them by walking up to them, we could sure do it with a lasso. Dick, being little and stooped anyway, his legs bowed and bent from a lifetime of riding, and his experience having been mostly with old spoiled or outlaw horses, where his worst fears were usually justified, had formed habits of handling his horse "from the ground up" so to speak. When he went to catch a horse that we had walked up to for years, he would walk to within ten or fifteen feet of it, then start aiming at the hobbles, never looking at the horse at all, surely never looking it in the eye as we had always done, but sneaking up on the hobbles.

When he arrived, almost on all fours, he carefully undid the hobbles, then raised up to catch the horse. Our old saddle-horses got onto that real fast, and when the hobble flipped loose from the first leg, the horse whirled and was gone. This had the man at a bad disadvantage because when a horse whirled, it was natural to kick; we jumped back, which scared the horse, making it harder to get up to him again.

The situation of unhobbling a horse on the open range deteriorated from a common, rather personal rite of bringing some relief to the horse, to a contest of caginess between us. After Dick had been there a few years, sneaking up on the hobbles was the only way we could get up to a horse on the range, and if we could talk to him and rise up and put our hands on his neck and catch him, we both knew it was only because the horse was being permissive.

We all recognized that Dick was a scrap of surviving history, that he was the typical old Texas trailherd hand left over from the drives north, and we appreciated him as such. He smoked Prince Albert, but he rolled his "pills" in a novel manner. He would select a tan-colored cigarette paper—oh! I can see his brown hands so plainly in my mind's eye, gnarled and scarred from years of handling ropes and other rough tools on the range—from the packet of Riz la Croix "wheat" papers. From this he tore off about a quarter of an inch from the end and one side. Holding the paper in his left hand, which also held the can of tobacco, he would roll these tiny scraps of paper in his right thumb and fingers, moisten them on his tongue and roll them into a tight ball, which he flipped away. All this time, he would have us spell-bound with some story, his startlingly beautiful gray eyes, black-lashed, darting glances up from time to time.

He would then take his can of tobacco and pour a scanty measure into his abbreviated paper, roll it expertly and moisten it on his tongue, "tighten" it, then smooth it into a slim, exact cigarette, which he called a cigareet.

He inhaled deeply, while drinking sips of black coffee from a granite or tin cup which he had balanced on a coal or two from the campfire. His coffee simmered all the time, but he supped it carefully, and we just assumed that since he had been doing this since his childhood way back there in the dim past, his gullet was probably parboiled and without feeling by this time.

Dick developed an outfit on the Arizona Strip, which he tended from time to time, but when he got too old to punch cows as he had done in the past, he sold out and spent the rest of his years in retirement. He lived in Kingman, Arizona, in the winters, returning to Cortez, Colorado, for a while in the summer, where he stayed at the hotel and just visited with his old friends as they strayed past.

One summer when Noel, my youngest son, was about twelve-years-old, I was selling Minnesota Woolens so that I could wander around, and we picked Dick up and made a trip to Mesa Verde Park. We camped in the public camp ground, and when Dick started the breakfast fire by tearing off some chunks of cedar bark and ripping off a few tree limbs,

I cringed, hoping we would not get caught. He told Noel to take some eggshells and throw them off the cliff, but that I stopped, tactfully, and we put them into the garbage can.

During the morning, we wandered around, and found that the horse wrangler with horses tied up for the tourists to take rides on was an old *compadre* of Dick's. We left him there, since he couldn't walk very far and thought it was beneath his horseman dignity to do it anyway, while we covered the park.

When we returned there had been a change in Dick. He had had the word from his friend, and after that he was most scrupulous about where and how he got kindling, and what he did with garbage, and he watched Noel and me carefully that we didn't break the rules.

He added so much to the trip for us; he had been raised in that country, and had camped all one winter in one of the caves wherein the cliff dwellers had left some of their most interesting ruins. The boys could hardly have cared less— let the cliff dwellers tend to their own business and the cowboys would follow suit some two or three centuries later.

They didn't even explore the caves, they were interested only in the shelter the one cave gave their camp from the severe winter storms. He told us, also, that in riding the range in that heavily cedared country, a man would often break out into a clearing that had once been farmed by the Indians, and often would stumble over the ruins of adobe houses. Some of these have been found, but undoubtedly there are thousands that have not been, and some that will never be discovered.

Dick's vocabulary was as colorful as his personality. He couldn't sleep on bright moonlight nights—the full moon gave him the "blare eye." Since I can't think offhand of any more of his sayings, in all likelihood they have fallen into our vocabularies until they are ours. He was a story teller *de luxe,* and we

listened to his tales avidly, told in the vernacular we understood. He had ridden with the Indians of southwestern Colorado all his life, and his gesture, his very.stance, partook of
that flavor. Privately we considered his sneaking up on a horse
had been learned from his red brethren.

Dick taught me something else—to hobble my stirrups
when I rode a horse I thought might unload me. This means
tying the stirrups together under the horse's belly, pulling them
down against him tightly if you are really going to use them,
but letting them out a bit if you need only a little help. Tightly
hobbled stirrups are rough to ride with, you can't "stand up
in your stirrups" at all, and they kink your knees uncomfort-
ably. But if you need them—Ah! nothing else in the world
gives you the purchase those hobbled stirrups do when you sit
down tight in the saddle and push against them! You'd better
take all the advantage you can; if you get piled, you leave
under such pressure that it is like squirting a melon seed; you
might not come down until fall.

I rode one mule with hobbled stirrups. She was so quick
and treacherous, and I was so scared of her that I figured
I needed the advantage. Which was true, but I'd come in at
night virtually a cripple.

Around 1920 we got a whole new set of neighbors. Well,
only Andy Moore at North Springs was new; Lou Chaffin and
his family took cattle Under the Ledge and Tidwells moved
onto the High part of the Spur.

Tidwells beat my Uncle Offie to the Spur by an eyelash.
We were taking a trough down to put in the Big Spring there
when we cut their cow tracks in Horseshoe Canyon. Since we
never considered the High Part of the Spur our range, it was
all right with us, and we just put the trough in at Outlaw
Seep, which otherwise probably would never have been developed because it was so small and near the Big Tank. Uncle

Offie moved to the Burr Desert, across the Dirty Devil River, but quit the cow business a few years later and never went back to it.

Clyde Tidwell, the oldest of the boys, ran the outfit since Delbert, Leland and Adolph were younger. The father, Frank Tidwell, and the brother older than Delbert had died during the flu epidemic of 1918 while Clyde was in the Service. Clyde was a half-brother, his father had been killed by an accidental gun-shot when the young couple and baby were coming west in a covered wagon. His mother taught school for a year or so then married Frank Tidwell. Clyde was so young, that he grew up under the Tidwell name.

Dolphie was about my age, and the other two were older. They all worked for us off and on for the next seven or eight years.

Lou Chaffin had three sons, also, Fawn, Ken and Clell. His two younger boys, Ned and Gay, rode with the cattle in later years, but in that time of 1920-25, the former three were around our place a lot. Fawn was older, but Ken and Clell were about Hazel's and my age, and with Dolphie we considered ourselves the five invincibles. We had more fun than kids really are entitled to, and we often included the older fellows.

I remember we played mumbly-peg—our version of it, with a knife whose handles sported naked women under the celluloid handles. When the knife had been new, this must have been most daring, but by the time Hazel acquired it somehow, the celluloid had become so scratched that even close study failed to reveal much. The knife was sacred to us not because of its pornographic interest, but because it was the official mumbly-peg knife.

There was a regular series of moves wherein the knife had to be stuck up in the sand of the arena enclosed by our legs as we squatted tailor-fashion in a circle.

I think we began by tossing the knife into the center of the ring, then we had "pickin's" made by placing the point of the knife between the tips of our thumb and first the index finger then on down the rest, tipping it off to stick up in the sand. If it fell over, the knife went to the next player; if it stuck up, but slanted doubtfully, the player carefully removed the sand from under the handle until only the blade was buried. If the knife still held, it was called a good throw. The last move of the game was "Overhead and out!" It was every man for himself, and the contest waged loudly and bitterly, but all in fun; no one ever got sore about it.

In the winter of 1922-23, Dolphie was working for my father when he got sick. His brother Delbert took him to town in the wagon, where they caught the train for Salt Lake City, picking up their mother at Wellington. Dolphie had a ruptured appendix, which would be rather simple to handle with the miracle drugs of today, but he died a day or two after reaching the hospital.

This disrupted our group; never again did we have such fun. We all grew up a bit and gave over our childish games. Ken and Clell were around, and we enjoyed them, but I don't think we ever played mumbly-peg after that, and somehow things were different.

Our friendship with the Chaffin boys never extended to town social life. For some reason, they never considered us girl friends, and we never went out with them. I think my mother resented this, but I doubt we girls did; they were too much like brothers to us.

My father was without any formal education, he could barely write his own name, but my mother was a wide reader and had there been a library handy, we would have been a well informed family. However, my father was interested in everything, and had a fine memory. We often discussed abstract topics, lending what information we had to the situation. I remember three subjects that engendered a good bit of opinion, pro and con, but only one of which I have ever been able to resolve.

The one I have solved is the "sound" one. It goes: If a limb breaks off a tree in the forest and there is no living thing to hear it, does it make a sound? Of course, the answer lies in the definition of *sound*. If it is defined as something heard, and nothing hears it, then obviously it didn't make a sound; if the definition is the resultant noise of a physical action, then whether or not an ear catches it, there is a sound.

The other two are (1) does it rain toads and (2) what is a horsehair snake. I have actually seen the ground covered with tiny toads after a downpour, and where they came from, I have no way of knowing. If they had been larger, I could have believed they were buried in the ground until the rain brought them to the surface—but really tiny, just-out-of-the-pollywog stage? Forget it!

Occasionally, but very rarely, we found a horsehair snake in a tank of clear water. They might have been in the red rain-water tanks, but if so, we couldn't have seen them. They looked like fat, black horse hairs—like a hair from a horse's tail, maybe fifteen or twenty inches long that had been well soaked up. They were twirled in loops around sticks, or lay in a sort of tangle. If we took a twig and raked them out of the water, they writhed and twined around the stick. We never did dissect one to see what it was like inside; we never killed anything, but now I sort of wish we had.

The argument raged whether these were in truth horse hairs with some sort of life, or were they a kind of worm. How did they acquire life, or propagate? I still don't know, and when I find someone who had ever heard of them, he doesn't know, either.

This argument usually tailed off by the believers accusing the unbelievers of not having faith in anything. "Why you probably don't even believe in hoop-snakes!" was supposed to be the final, crushing blow. We had been raised on the old whopper of the hoop snake that takes its tail in its mouth and rolls down hills. It is very venomous, and once it bit Grandfather's wagon tongue, which swelled up until it broke the ring in the neckyoke.

Our fun was home-made, but it was real. Don't ever think that our active life was anything but most interesting.

Hazel, about twelve, a real hand and she shows it.

The only picture I have of us as kids. Far left is Leland Tidwell, then Hazel with Ken wading farther out. Dolphie has just walked up to Clell.

12

Growing Up

One time (in 1919) Mama, Hazel and I took a camping trip; we went down Horseshoe Canyon to the Indian Paintings. Papa helped us pack the mule that morning, but after that we were on our own for the next three mornings, the time we planned to spend exploring.

When somone asks me if I think that Butch Cassidy and his Wild Bunch left any caches at the Roost or in the canyons, I admit that he very well might have; we were always too busy to hunt treasure. This trip we dedicated to leisure and exploration.

There were pictographs everywhere in the canyons,* but

---

*This Indian Rock Art consists of pictographs or petroglyphs or a combination of both. There is no doubt that some of them give instructions or directions for trails or waterholes, but some of them seem to be ritualistic or even historical in nature, and others seem to be purely a form of creative art. They never have any pornographic hint.

These ancient artists covered a tremendous range of animals, reptiles and insects in their figures, but there is one omission that puzzles me: Nowhere in the southwest have I ever seen a fish depicted. Fish drawings are common in the northwest, but in Utah, New Mexico, Arizona and Nevada, there is not one that I have ever seen or heard about. When I mention this to archeologists, it gives them pause, but no one has offered an explanation.

Since these paintings antedate the Navajo legend of the fish taboo, I can't accept this as the reason. This legend is:

the ones in Horseshoe (Barrier Creek) were the biggest and plainest, covering a big stretch of the canyon wall. Today, people come from all over the world to look at them, sometimes driving to the bottom of the canyon on the Phillips Oilrig road, from where they have to get back out of the canyon on the opposite side onto the Spur, since the bottom half-mile of the road going in is down a sandy hillside which no car on earth can pull back up. Actually, the best plan is to leave the car out of the canyon and walk down, being sure to go far enough up the canyon to see the best pictographs

These have become known as the Barrier Canyon style, with the figures wedge-shaped and dressed in elaborate robes. Some of them have headdresses, some of them don't; some have arms, either proportionate to the figures or very small; and some of the pictures show just the wedge-shaped body.

One group tells a story, a man shoots an elk. I guess it is an elk, it seems to have too much horn for a deer. Most of the dogs have six toes on each foot, and the sheep look like Desert Bighorn sheep. Several different shades of "paint" were used, from a dark brownish red which shows plainly, to a buff red almost as light as the canyon wall on which they were painted, and there was some white paint used. In all probability the paint was made from clays mixed with sheep fat. It seems to me that the figures are not as bright as they were forty or fifty years ago, but I can't tell for sure.

During the uranium mining days of the 1940s, a fellow had a crew of Navajo miners. One Sunday this fellow went fishing, throwing his catch up on the bank until he had quite a number of fish of various kinds, catfish, suckers, etc., which abounded in the San Juan River.

Some of the Indians came down to see what he was doing, and they were simply appalled when they learned he was planning to eat the fish. They showed their contempt of the fish every way they could, kicking sand on them and spitting (although, not on the fish), and making sounds of disgust. They told him that a long time ago their fathers had chased the Moquis into the river (the Colorado) where they had turned into fish. Therefore, eating fish horrified them. But there seemed to be overtones of contempt about them, too, a sort of superstitious repugnance.

The afternoon we rode down the canyon, taking our own sweet time about it, a nice summer rain came. Oh, the miracle of rain on the desert! The exquisite, sensuous joy of it. Every sense is delighted, not only is the dust washed from the trees, from the very earth! but also the air is fresh crystal. Every blade of grass is shining, every leaf stands out individually immaculate, every rock and cliff and mesa glows with new clarity, and the whole scene is bathed in fresh color, new as first creation.

And the smells—oh, the wonderful odor of wet sage and cedar, the subtle aromas of grasses and brush and trees, and the freshly opened flowers throw out veritable skeins of perfume to tempt the wandering bee. The very earth smells alive again.

Across the suddenly purified distance heavenly sounds drift seemingly for miles—plash of water that has been too-long forgotten, bird songs that are paeans of thanksgiving and the rarer, more subtle voices of the other small folk of the suddenly teeming desert add their under-chords until the world hums with sheer delight.

The very air has substance; it can be felt against the skin not as weightless atmosphere, but as a caress of emolience. Suddenly one is wrapped in living radiance of euphoria.

The rain has come! Once again life is sweet on the tongue, and God is near and good!

The miracle was thrice blessed in the canyon. No longer were the walls sheer and harsh, the sand loose and abrasive under our feet. A soft glow filled the chasm, and the sand was cool and firm. The sound of running, splashing water was magnified a thousand times by the hundreds of waterfalls cascading over every low notch of the canyon walls—and the water was all a beautiful ocher red from the brilliant Carmel formation above. And the spray was *pink!*

We camped that night part way to the paintings, early

enough to get our horses taken care of and supper over so that we could climb up on the canyon rims. It was so wonderful to be free to do exactly as we wished.

We camped at the paintings the next night so that we could have both morning and evening light for pictures, this being the purpose of our visit. The sun cooperated, and we did all right.

The next day we came back past the Sidehill Spring in Spur Canyon, and took our time climbing up to it to look it over carefully, a treat we had promised ourselves for years.

Somewhere in the canyon—I can't recollect exactly where, but I do remember it was on this trip—we found more of the lovely purplish-pink wild sweet peas. The only other patch I can recall is on a sandhill of the Upper Pasture. These grew in a sparse tangle on the blow-sand dune, and the blooms, larger than tame sweet peas, blotched with pink and dark purple, smelled heavenly. They didn't last long after we picked them for our hatbands, but they were lovely indeed. They came only in wet years or after a rain, and I doubt they have been seen for forty years.

Nothing much actually happened on this trip, but we remembered it with pleasure for years, and our pictures were the first of the thousands and thousands that have been taken of the Barrier Canyon Galleries.

When I was in my teens we bought our first truck. My mother had been stricken with appendicitis and Papa hauled her to town on the wagon. Remember the Roost is still 75 (country!) miles from Green River. She went on to the hospital and had her appendix removed, but it scared Papa. Up to that time, he had never considered that he might have to take any of the family out for medical attention and that he would need speedier transportation than a horse. So they bought a Ford truck, specially equipped to travel over the sand.

Lou Chaffin called it "The Ship of the Desert," and he

admired it very much—but then he didn't have to cope with it. It had Warford and Ruxtell auxiliary gears, which gave it some fifteen speeds forward and about five in reverse. The brakes were minimal, and we geared down to descend the steep dugways made for wagons, but if we missed getting the Warford in gear, everything was out—no brakes, no gears, no anything; and those dugways were sometimes long and crooked and always narrow.

My father didn't trust this vehicle at all, and never did learn to drive it. He always sent one of us kids along on a horse, leading a horse for him. The truck had a hand feed for gas, and I shudder yet to remember that he always did the gas feeding when he rode with us. Sometimes this just didn't get the job done very well, two drivers did not always see the constant road hazards in exactly the same light. Mama foxed him, finally, when she learned there was such a thing as a foot-feed and had one installed.

One time they were taking a load of oats out to the Nougier Ranch on San Rafael where it could be picked up by wagon or pack for use on the desert, and Mama goofed the Warford at the top of the dugway going down onto the benches. The truck careened down the narrow, steep road, Mama guiding it desperately, as best she might, not much scared since she had met the situation before. But Papa was petrified—he thought they were in imminent danger of being crushed by the heavy load or dashed over the ledges into a gully—which was not too far from the truth. Finally she missed a turn, the truck scooted up on the sidehill until it ran out of momentum then it tipped over. Papa asked Mama if she was hurt, and when she said she wasn't instead of opening his door (which was uppermost) and getting out, he upped with his bootheel and demolished the windshield. This made Mama sore, and when Joe Motte arrived on the scene shortly after, the situation was somewhat tense.

Betsy, as we called her, was used to freight supplies out from town, going by way of the mouth of San Rafael and Keg Springs, up the long Antelope Valley, then over into the Cedars, and finally topping out onto the Roost Flats where danger of getting stuck in the sand was all behind, and the rest of the trip home pure joy ride. This was the only feasible route, and while there was plenty of sand on it, not nearly as much as on any other route. The CCC (Civilian Conservation Corps) boys built a grade topped with hardpan clay and gravel from the Hanksville road through the Flat Tops and up Sweetwater Hill onto the gravel North Springs benches, which is the road used today.

About the time we got Betsy, Chaffins developed the ranch at the mouth of San Rafael and the Texas and Phillips petroleum companies drilled wells at the top of Sweetwater Hill and on the Spur, so that considerable work was done on the road. The sand was never really conquered, and is still an item, although cars are much improved and low-pressure tires much more sandworthy than the pnuematic tires Betsy used, although we did have what we called balloon tires on the rear wheels.

The road through the Cedars was the worst; that sand was just bottomless, and during the hard spring winds, the tracks would whip full as fast as the loose sand could be cleared out. This stretch of road was virtually impassable.

Clayt Kofford, the government trapper, once made an early spring reconnaisance trip to the Roost and hit the sand at its dry worst and the spring winds at their highest. It took him and his boss a day and a half to go a mile and a half through the Cedars. Finally out on the Roost Flats he was home in a breeze, but he never quit telling about the sand in the Cedars.

My father believed that the car resting its weight on the tires was hard on them, so when we were not using the truck, it was parked under the saddle shed and jacked up on blocks.

Thus, we didn't use it nearly as much as we would have if it had been handier. It was easier to saddle a horse and ride over to Twin Corrals to see if the pond had received any water from the storm he had watched so hopefully, or for any other errand. Going to the Roost Spring was always on horseback; Betsy never could have pulled herself up out of the heavy going of the Roost Draw.

In our early teens we girls discovered the advantages Levis had over the bib overalls we had worn up to then. We never did wear anything else to ride in after that. We were a generation ahead of our time, and much looked down on for wearing pants, but we were innocent of trying to be boys— we just had learned how comfortable and handy Levis were. They stayed down on our legs when we rode fast (stood up in our stirrups, as we put it), with the rub coming on the overall leg rather than the skin. This was an item; we always rode fast. They stayed down over our boot tops, too, and didn't let twigs and boughs fall in if we were cedar-popping after wild cattle, and they were tough enough to protect our knees against the brush, too.

Another advantage was pockets. From our bib-overall pockets we had lost about everything we ever tried to carry, but from a Levi pocket, you had to need something badly for it to be worth the effort to dig it out. We carried knives, whetstones, matches and buckskin strings just like all the rest of the riders, and it was an advantage to be able to produce these necessaries.

We also wore riding boots—I guess you can say we were two generations ahead in those. I feel at last vindicated to have the world accept something that we knew all the time, and that we received considerable criticism for adopting. It's tough to be an innovator—no one agrees with you or gives you any credit for discovery.

Our boots were hand made to measure, and came mostly

from Hyer in Olathe, Kansas. Blucher boots were worn, too, but they were made grain side out and didn't wear as well as Hyers. These were made flesh-side out and while they couldn't scuff, you couldn't have polished them if you had wanted to. It took them months, or maybe even years, to wear slick, but they sure were tough and comfortable. Besides giving needed support to ride in, boots were fun to walk in. You just can't walk any other way but proud in boots, no matter how beat up they are. You know all the time you are set apart—superior.

I remember one new pair I was breaking in. They were made to measure and fit like a second skin, but the new leather had more "draw" than a mustard plaster. I'd start out in the morning pretty fancy in my new boots, but before noon they would get to drawing and I'd take them off and finish the day barefoot.

We were riding the Gordons, and I had taken all the joshing I was going to; I vowed I would ride all that day in those boots if it killed me. On the way back that afternoon past Frenchy, I wasn't too sure of the outcome. I was in mortal agony but not saying a word. In fact, I was riding with locked jaws, afraid to try to speak lest I start screaming.

My horse walked up to the trough at Frenchy, and suddenly I saw something new to try. I piled off and stepped over into the icy water on the trough in those boots. I tell people I actually heard them sizzle and saw steam come up, and no one believes me, but I believe it.

And the relief—the heavenly, exquisite, instant relief! I sloshed around a few minutes, not daring to accept the change. Of course my feet were dry, those boots were beautifully hand made; they would never have leaked a drop of water. When I got back on my horse I was comfortable, and they never "drew" again; they were nothing but comfort for years and years.

Our cash crop was steers, and we delivered them to the railroad at Green River about June 1. We sold them at yearlings, with a few twos missed the year before. Sometimes there were older ones, but with the constant riding my father did, they were few indeed. Delivery day of the first of June was set because that was the time the cattle could be put on the high forest ranges where they were taken for the summer. In the fall, they were then shipped to Denver or Kansas City for feeding out on midwestern farms.

Steers were sold ahead of time—contracted—but the old cows shipped in the fall were just put on the market. Actually steers were our bread and butter product, old cows being a sort of bonus—either we sold them or they died in the winter, so they were salvage.

Bill Schumm of Gypsum, above Glenwood Springs, Colorado, bought our steers for several years, and put them on the Coffee Pot range for the summer. Mama, Papa and Hazel spent some time one summer as his guests on the mountain, and I made a trip or two up there. It was a really beautiful mountain range in the top of the Colorado Rockies, and we enjoyed the forest and streams to the utmost.

The last few years he lived my father didn't wean his calves in the fall, believing that the cow had more "heart" for the winter if she was mothering a calf, and that she and the calf lay close together and furnished each other some warmth. The amount of milk she gave didn't make much difference to her, but it did to the calf. In those days, the snow was much deeper than it has been the past 30 years, and that makes a difference in how cattle are handled.

In the spring he was abroad mighty early to catch the few yearlings that the cows had not "kicked off" before the new calves came. Usually a cow would not let the yearling suck for a month or so before the new calf was due, but if she didn't follow this instinct, she often became so attached to the big hulk she let it have all the milk and the baby calf starved to death.

As we gathered the steers into the pasture for holding to sell, of course we weaned them; we also held any yearling heifers that needed weaning. Early in the roundup each day's ride brought in some of these "pairs" as we called them. When we had gathered enough to make a drive to the holding pasture, we cut the cows out and held the yearlings in the corral overnight. The cows with yearling calves, some twenty or thirty of the hundred or so we were holding, tramped around and around the corral on the outside, followed on the inside by the calves, both setting up a clamor.

The next morning, we rounded up the cows and shoved them up the road toward Sunflower Valley, giving them a real start. Then we ran back to the corral, jerked the gate open and while one rider went in to whip out the drags, the rest of the crew rode point, just keeping the calves in a bunch and letting them run out past the pond and up the draw until they were somewhat winded, when they were willing to slow down and be herded. If we had tried to hold them up before, they would have just spilled in every direction, but by keeping them together and letting them get their run over with, we managed to hang onto them until we could convince them we had the situation in hand.

We drove them to Twin Corrals and dropped over into Horseshoe Canyon where we usually hazed them along to either the Upper or Lower Pasture. Thus the weaners were behind a fence or two and couldn't return, although they tried. The cows bawled around the corral for a day or two then wandered off.

A few days before delivery time (counted carefully) we swept the canyon, including the Pastures, to below the Sandslide. On the proper day, we gathered the herd and trimmed it. My father always did all the cutting out, never allowing any other man in the herd. I have seen more than one man cutting a herd, but it creates a mess; it chouses the cattle unnecessarily and excites them until they are so much harder to handle that considerable effort and time are lost.

Papa strove for a uniform looking bunch of steers, cutting back a few of the best ones as well as the tag end. A steer buyer always cut back a few—it was expected—so we left a few of the tag tail to get rid of in that way, six or eight pretty scroungy calves. These were then sold to the buyer at a reduced price.

We turned the herd up the Sandslide, where they grazed and wandered to the top. Cows like to climb, and will go up a trail quite willingly that they have to be forced down step by step. The next morning we picked the horses we were going to use, gathered up the steers, 250 to 350 head, and took them out the Sandslide Trail and across Blue John Canyon, emerging in the Cedars that bordered the north edge of Roost Flats. These cattle had seen the last of the Roost.

The first night we held at North Springs, or in later years when we had more cattle to consider, in the head of Middle Canyon. The next day the herd was on the trail at first light, down North Springs Wash, over the Black Ridge at the Gap, where a noon rest left time for the crew to have lunch. Then down the long slope to San Rafael, veering off to the mouth of Spring Canyon below Dugout, where the crossing was better. The river was in full flood, swimming deep.

When the cattle smelled water and quickened their pace, Papa and another rider fell in lead and held them back while the rest of the crew fanned up the drags. The herd hit the river at a good clip and were forced in and across before they really knew what was going on. Let a cow drink and start back and you don't get her across the river without a fight, but while the whole outfit is still bent on getting a drink, shove them out into swimming water and on across, then let them drink and they wander away on that side perfectly content.

We always laid over a day on the San Rafael to let the cattle rest and fill up. The next drive was to Cottonwood Bottom on the Green River, where the cattle drank from the river and grazed on the limited, ledge-enclosed river bottom.

The next day we hit the railroad stock yards about noon or early in the afternoon. The old stock yards were in the center of town, north and east of the depot. This meant that the wild cattle had to cross the tracks west of town, come down where the airport is today, on down past the depot and finally end up in the corrals. It was an exciting trip for the cattle, the riders and the townsmen.

Later the stock yards were built south of the tracks out on the bank of the Salaratus Wash. It was a bad place to corral wild cattle, they had to go forward toward all that was strange, and the brush and wash banks made horsemanship a catty business to overcome the reluctance of the herd and force it along.

Mama always got away as quick as she could and went to the closed, dusty house to don a dress and start housekeeping again. But we girls were not averse to showing off our horsemanship a bit although we never would have admitted it.

The packs were unloaded into the granary behind the house, and the horses watered at the ditch and fed their grain. Then, after the cattle were loaded into the cars that evening, and were tallied and paid for, came our yearly vacation. We girls renewed our friendships in the town, Mama got all the bills paid and supplies bought, Papa visited with his cronies and likely as not traveled somewhere to look for bulls, and we considered the year finished.

This was the high point, the reason for the whole operation, and it was much enjoyed. We rode our "tops" to town, and they and we stepped a bit proudly.

One morning a few days after delivery, the glory faded and we threw on our saddles and packs and set out on a whole new year, with the branding ride just ahead. My father would lead out, my mother followed loyally and unquestioningly, and the whole operation fell into a rhythm of good management that is a privilege to look back upon.

In about 1945, Hazel and I began to see that some of the most interesting stories of the West were not being recorded, so we begged Mama to write some of these and put them into a loose leaf notebook for us for Christmas. We had in mind some of the things that we could remember, but mostly Mama copied her diaries of trips she had had, which were more exciting to her than the daily routine at the Roost. However, she did come up with two or three that made it all worth while. Together with her poem about the Roost, we had a sample of what her life had been. This material has been included here:

Joe didn't carry a gun much. The Roost country was sandy and Joe was a big man and always had a heavy saddle. Sometimes he put the 30:30 on the kids' saddles but they were never handy when he needed the gun and they "beefed" if he didn't get it right and it rubbed their legs. So almost always we rode without a gun.

There were more coyotes then and seems like they must have been meaner. We often found calves killed and sometimes one with his ham eaten out or his tail nipped off. We surely hated the coyotes and put out poison baits and Joe never passed a chance to rope one. He had a big, brown horse, Browney, that we raised, that would tromp a coyote if he got close enough. Very handy, but it had its disadvantages; he served the dogs the same.

One time when we were riding Antelope Valley I was up on a hill and Joe jumped a coyote. I had a good view. He was riding Old Chub. They started down the trail making twenty-one and picking it up. The coyote would dodge and Joe and Chub would turn and take him again. Chub wasn't as handy as Browney, but he was gaining and the coyote was getting tired. Joe shook out a loop and looked like it wouldn't last much longer when Chub bowed his head and started to buck. Joe was spurring pretty hard but wasn't looking for that and was pretty busy for a few minutes. When he got things straightened out the coyote had disappeared and he couldn't find it. He was pretty upset because I couldn't say where the coyote had gone. Golly, with a show like that, I should watch a *coyote!*

Once she described killing a "b'ar":

We used to live at the Roost in the summer and move to Green River for school in the fall. We never wanted to go very much and Joe hated to see us go. He always killed a beef for us to take, because, he said, the fresh fruit and vegetables wouldn't make us sick if we had plenty of meat. It didn't either, and something must have saved us a good belly-ache for we'd surely tank up.

In 1921 we had a four-horse team, and it took us two and a half days to go to town. It takes three to four hours now with a car.

When we got to Dugout, a wash draining into San Rafael just below Harris Bottoms, the kids decided to walk for a while. There were a few cattle along the water there, and the girls wanted to walk down the wash while the road went along the side and sometimes over out of sight of the wash. Joe told them to watch for cattle that were ours; I think he just taught them to be alert that way, because he could tell if a cow was his at quite a distance—we used to say "as far as he could see one."

The cattle were all either red or Herefords in those days, and suddenly Pearl said, "There's a black one! Oh, it's a *bear!*"

Sure enough, it was, although it was a long way from bear range, had drifted down the San Rafael River from the mountains, we decided. We were all very excited, although Joe didn't make the fuss we did.

This was early September, and the day was awful hot. The bear, a little yearling brown one, ran across the wash and up under a ledge on the other side of the wash, where there was a spot of shade. Joe jerked the lead ropes off the horses and tied them together for a lasso, and took old Babe, one of the leaders, a big roan horse, out of the harness. The kids got the ax out of the load, and I got the Kodak. We went around on the ledge above the bear.

Joe got off the horse and dropped a loop over the lip of the ledge, but the bear dodged it with his head, and the old tie ropes were limp and tangled anyhow, but he caught its hind foot. The bear decided to move on, but Joe jerked up the slack and started to pull him up. I was off to the side about thirty feet taking pictures as fast as I could, but I was so excited they were not very good, when the bear turned in mid-air, caught the rope with his front foot and started to come back up the rope. I dropped the camera and ran to hand Joe the ax—the kids were there by him and things went so fast we never did agree who handed it to him. We held the rope then and Joe swung at the bear with the ax. The first blow didn't stop him, and we were ready to drop the rope and run, but the second blow knocked him back limp.

We dressed him out and threw him on the wagon to take along. We had often eaten bear meat, and found it delicious, and this was a yearling cub and should be good eating. We were headed for the old Nougier Ranch about twelve miles above Harris Bottom, where the Dan Gillies family lived. When we arrived, Rosa (Mrs. Gillies) and I went down to the garden, and Joe skinned the bear. When we came back, Joe had left the feet on, and it just looked terrible to us—remember we had calf meat—so we just didn't care for bear meat.

Then there was the bob-cat:

We visited Neil Hanks at Nine Mile once and he gave us a few chickens. They were all colors and kinds and we loved them. We fixed a coop for them, taught them where the water was at the pond, set up some feeders and went riding off to be gone a week or so on the Spur or Gordons. When we returned, we had only one old white hen left, and she was a sorry looker; her feathers were most all gone and she had taken to the trees, as wild as she could be.

Joe looked at all the tracks around and decided that a bob cat had paid the chickens an extended visit. We killed the hen, but didn't enjoy eating her much because we hated to be out of the chicken business.

Early that fall Joe was coming down the trail near the cabin, returning from a ride not finished because he got sick, when a bob-cat ran down the trail ahead of him.

Joe was riding Poison, a big spooky sorrel horse, that hit the ground so hard when he ran that someone said he was "crotch bound." This brought out the remark that the rider had better be, too, or he would wind up split. Joe had no gun, his first thought of roping the cat was cut short by a twisting cramp in his stomach. Then memory wrangled the chickens.

He was fast at making a loop and soon caught the cat. When it felt the rope, it whirled and ran for Joe, who was remembering what happened when a bob-cat got on behind Joed Swasey. Fleetingly he wondered what Poison would do; he hit hard enough when he was just loping; no telling *how* hard he could buck.

Joe ran under a dry tree, throwing the rope over a limb as he went past and catching it on the other side, thus hanging the cat.

The chickens were avenged!

Mama also wrote poetry:

ROBBERS ROOST

In the eastern end of Wayne County,
    There is a lovely spring;
The Robbers Roost is its name,
    To it fond memories cling.
One drink of it, you lose your hope,
    Two, your religion's gone
Three, you want to rob a bank
    Before another dawn.

Old Blue John and old Silver Tip
    Lived there for many years,
They spent a very busy time, and
    Uncle Sam shed tears.

Dick Westwood took a bunch of men
   And to the Roost he went;
He caught those rogues with greatest ease,
   And to the Pen they went.

But Richard made a sad mistake,
   Amid the others' laughter,
He from this noted spring did drink,
   Had trouble ever after.
One drink of it, you lose your hope,
   Two, your religion's gone,
Three, you want to rob a bank
   Before another dawn.

Buhr, and Moore and Jack Cottrell
   All passed in quick succession,
Sanford, Walker and Cassidy,
   Were all in the procession.
For many years it was alone,
   Then Wild and Swasey came,
With pony and a jackass bunch,
   And made this place their home.

Now Joe Biddlecome is the one,
   Using these noted waters,
He lives out at the Robbers Roost
   With his wife and daughters.
The best of men have worked for Joe,
   And its the same each time,
After they have worked awhile,
   They all go down the line.

Now when you ride up to this spring,
   And start to get a drink,
A sign hangs there in right plain sight,
   To make you pause and think.
One drink of it you lose your hope,
   Two, your religion's gone,
Three, you want to rob a bank,
   Before another dawn.

MILLIE BIDDLECOME (1925)

Mama sitting on a calf's head while Papa brands it.
Hazel has just caught one and is taking up the slack.

13

Hobbies—Rawhide and Horsehair Work

JOE BIDDLECOME LIKED to make things, he had a definite artistic drive which he expressed with material at hand, turning out something of beauty or usefulness or often both. He always had a blacksmith shop, and his bridle bits and spurs were much sought after, particularly the bits. They were light and comfortable for a horse, with a wide loop in the center of the mouthpiece so that a horse couldn't cut its tongue if it fell and rammed the side pieces of the bit into the ground. Nor could a rider hurt a horse's mouth or tongue with these bits; I have seen horses with terribly scarred tongues from spade or other inhumane bits. With a Biddlecome bit a child could handle any horse with very little pressure.

My mother didn't ride with one of Papa's bits. One spring she bought herself a bit, a light, easy bit, with side pieces molded in the shape of a woman's leg—very daring. Papa was always giving his handiwork away, and more than likely he had given her bit to someone, and she bought this one to replace it before he got around to make her another one. It was a good one, light and comfortable for the horse, and she never used anything else. My son, Noel, has it today, and it is one of his choicest possessions.

In his youth, my father was never hampered by tradition and he was most original in his approach to many subjects. This showed in his handiwork. He once fashioned a pair of spurs with the rowels crosswise. These looked funny, but they did have advantages; they didn't mark a horse up, and they didn't roll and let a pitching horse throw the rider. They did have one disadvantage, though.

In those days he was pretty apt to get a little ragged and threadbare around the edges after several months on the range. One time his boots were coming apart, with the sole loosened from the top around the boot toe. He was dragging a dead tree up to the camp for firewood when the horizontal rowel from the spur on the other foot stabbed into this crevice and not only tripped him, but almost tore the boot apart and all but sliced his foot in half. He got onto his feet, unbuckled the spurs and threw them as far as he could. He never went near them again, and didn't make another pair.

In making bridle bits, at first he made the bit in three pieces, the mouthpiece and two sides, then fastened them together by boring a hole in the side pieces and inserting the mouthpiece and riveting the ends. He welded some things, but welding was such a chancey project in a crude forge that he figured out a way to make a bit of one piece of steel, usually spring steel, the springs from railroad cars beings just right. After drawing the center of the bar down to make the mouthpiece, he pounded the ends in until the bar was thick enough, and split it on each end, into the mouthpiece. He cut off one of the split ends for the top of the side piece and bent it up, bending the other down and drawing it out for the shank of the bit.

Spur rowels were made of a flat piece of steel, a silver dollar being just the right size for a pattern, which was then cut into 16 points. Dragging through the sand of the Roost, a rowel would gradually wear out not only the pin that held it in the spur, but the hole would get bigger and bigger. New pins were not much of a problem, but filing out a new rowel was quite a job.

First, after the circle was cut out, lines were scored dividing it into halves, into quarters, with each quarter split and finally the eights also divided. Thus there would be 16 points. A hole was bored in the exact center, and the disc nailed to the flat end of an old wagon wheel spoke, which was then clamped in the shop vice. The spoke could be turned as work progressed, or the nail pried up and the rowel turned. One side was filed, then the rowel turned over and finished. I have heard that sometimes silver dollars were actually used, but we never did.

During the early years at the Roost when we were still shooting out tanks, building trails and doing other rock work, my father sharpened his own drill steel. A hammer drill was any length up to about two and a half feet, but a deeper hole, like the ones we used in shooting out the trail to Trail Spring, was put down with a churn drill, a piece of steel some six or eight feet long with a cutting face on each end.

These faces were made by pounding the heated drill flat so that it was a small fan-shaped cutting edge some one and a half or two inches from corner to corner. The drill steel was usually about an inch in diameter. After shaping, the metal was heated to a cherry red, the tip dipped into water about a quarter of an inch and held there for two or three seconds, then removed. The surface of the fan was cleaned by a couple of swipes with a file to make a shiney surface to watch the temper run down. When the colors were just right, the whole drill was doused in the tub of water. Too hard, it chipped; too soft and the thin corners of the fan were soon worn off. They wore off, anyway, and the face had to be re-shaped from time to time.

Considering that he cut all of his metal with a cold chisel and did his welding in a crude forge, it almost staggers the imagination what fun he could have had with a welding torch. His oldest grandson, Joe Baker (who was about a year and a half old when his grandfather died), has his own welding shop today. Do you suppose he often senses someone looking over his shoulder as he lays a particularly fine bead or makes a difficult or delicate weld?

Another material that was plentiful and could be worked up into things he needed was rawhide. He could always use another rope—hogstring—hackamore. The supply of raw material was virtually inexhaustible, since no beef hide was ever wasted. The animal to be slaughtered was often chosen for its hide; if the meat proved tough, we ate it anyway; our teeth were excellent. A good, even, hide from which he could fashion a particularly beautiful piece of equipment was hard to come by.

Hides from animals that he found dead were of no value, even if fresh enough to salvage. There was something about the blood vessels just under the skin not draining which damaged the hide, and if the animal was in poor condition, there wasn't enough oil in the hide to cut the glue.

He was so skillful at skinning a beef that he never scored a hide, but after he had to accept help or be labeled a sorehead, he insisted that the thin sheath of flesh against the skin over the ribs be skinned onto the hide, to be removed after the hide was stretched.

After the hide was removed it was treated with a couple of handfuls of salt and rolled up. The next morning it was staked out—on the granary floor at the Roost, but any place in the shade was OK. There was a school of thought that salt "burned" a hide, but Papa maintained that the sun burned a hide, and he always kept it in the shade.

In his early camps where there was no place to stretch a hide, he cut his strings while it was green, hanging the string outside, sun or no sun, until it was dry. In a day or two he could start carefully scraping the hair off the long strip with his pocket knife.

Cutting the green hide had another advantage; it was a bit hard to recognize a cow by the hide if that hide was in a long string. When they lived on Piñon Mesa, shortly after they were married, Papa butchered a big roan steer, absolutely the finest rawhide a man could get. The next morning, long after he had left for the day, Mama started toward the Utah Bottom with a quarter of beef for the home folks. While getting ready, she noticed the hide was really not out of sight under the roots of a tree near the cabin. The owner might come along at any time. She carried the heavy hide down the hill a short distance and really cached it under a big rock, with some other rocks placed strategically over it.

When she got back the next day, she almost had to rope her husband out of the cedars; he had come in the afternoon before a little early to cut his strings, and not finding the hide, deduced that the owner had it and he was in deep trouble. She never understood his lack of appreciation of her better hiding place.

Looking back, it seems to me I stretched a million hides on the granary floor, but it couldn't have been that many. I didn't mind doing it, and I did it satisfactorily, so for ten or fifteen years there were mighty few that I didn't stretch. I had a real "feeling" for rawhide and liked to work with it.

After the hide had partly dried, Papa "fleshed" it with the sharp edge of the end of a board. Actually, he just started the flesh loose and then pulled it off until the hide was clean. When it had dried thoroughly he took it up, rolled it hair side out and hung it up until he could get time to work on it. This was usually in the winter.

He took the hair off the whole hide with a sharp butcher knife. Unrolling the hide carefully so as not to bend and "break" the fibers, he laid it across a wagon tongue and, being careful not to cut the grain, scraped the hair off in long strokes.

Then he threw it into the reservoir and weighted it with rocks to soak thoroughly. From the dripping wet hide he cut his strings with his pocket knife, going around and around the hide from the outside edge until he was down to about a plate-sized piece. He was careful of two things: He kept the hide as nearly round as he could so the resultant string would stretch flat; a corner would have left a bad place in the string. And he carefully started his next cut in the end of the last one so that there were no nicks on the edges. That is why he used a knife; no amount of skill with any kind of scissors would have made a smooth-sided string.

Belly, flanks and legs of the hide were discarded, with only the best part used. Even then, it was never the same thickness. That over the neck was thicker than the best hide on the back and hips. Finally he figured out a way to gauge the thickness of his string. He drove a mower sickle blade into a slot cut out of a hardwood plank. He cut the slot just wide enough to accommodate the greatest width of his string, smoothed off the "threshold" of his slot, rounding it a bit so that when he drove the sickle blade down in the top, the string followed the slot up into the cutting edge.

He gauged for thickness first, and he ran the string through several times, cutting off the thinnest of slices until all of it touched the edge of the blade. He ran the string from one tub of water into another in this operation, and it took a steady hand not to let it "chatter" and cut unevenly. From this point he worked the rawhide in a dryer state, and he kept it scrupulously clean.

He gauged the string for width in another ingeniously simple device. He sawed a slanting cut into this same hardwood plank, cut the tip from this slot until the end on his side of the plank was just a little narrower than the outside. He stuck his pocket knife blade so that it cut into the top edge of wood in the slot, and the razor edge was away from him, almost straight with the edge of the string. Again, he cut several times, first on one side then on the other. When he finished, the string was exactly the same width and thickness from one end to the other. In this operation, he handled the rawhide almost dry, so that it couldn't stretch and squeeze through the slot, but would hold its form. To keep a little moisture in it, and make it soft enough to handle, he kept it wrapped in a damp gunnysack.

Then he beveled the string on all four edges, top and bottom, placing his knife blade in the slot of the plank at an angle, but cutting only the sharp edge of the rawhide off so that he still had a bit of thickness at the sides of the string. If the bevel was too deep, the side edges curled up in braiding and spoiled the appearance of the finished product. All of this was sheer drudgery, but it turned out an article of rope, hackamore nosepiece, hogstring of more than passing beauty.

I have seen only one other set of strings that equalled his, and those were cut and gauged by Herb Weber, when he lived on the Cat Ranch on the Henry Mountains in the late 1950s. They were really superb, and I was qualified to judge. I had done a whole bunch of that kind of work all the while I was growing up, and am probably the only living person who ever made a twisted rawhide rope.

Rawhide lariats (we called them lassos) were plaited (we called it braided) of four strings, and they "braided up" roughly a fourth; hackamore nosepieces about a third and quirts over a half. For a rope 40 feet long, the usual length, he needed four strings some 50 or 55 feet long or about 250 feet of string, all cut from the same hide, and it took a big hide and careful cutting to come out with that much. Anything over was sheer velvet, and he made the rope as long as he had string for.*

When my father's string was ready, just the right dampness, having been wrapped all night (at least) in a medium-damp gunny sack, he measured it into four strands the same length, still being careful not to let it get dirty or sandy, and "wrapped his skeins."

He worked on a large piece of tarp, and woe to the onlooker who kicked even a little sand on it! Having someone hold the end of a string, he ran it down through his left palm, turned his hand and hooked the string over his fingers, keeping it perfectly flat, but as loose as possible. Then he turned his hand back and wrapped it over his fingers the other way, using the string to turn his wrap on.

When he had finished, he had a neatly wrapped skein which he secured around the middle with the end of the string, after slipping his hand out. This would feed from the center, but maintain the unused string in a ball. As he braided, he had to keep the strings disentangled ahead of his braiding, which would have been impossible without winding them up some way.

Other than my father, the only man I ever saw braid a lasso was Delbert Tidwell. When he was a big kid staying at the ranch one summer, Papa showed him how to gauge strings, and he made a set and braided a rope. It took him all day just for the braiding, and although he wore gloves with the fingers cut off so he could manipulate the strings, while the palms protected his hands, he had a good set of blisters, and he was exhausted.

Rawhide is braided just a little damp—too wet and it

---

*There was always a range joke about the length of a man's lariat. If it was 35 feet or shorter, he rode fast horses; but if it coiled up on his saddle so that the other men could see it was much longer than that, he was either riding slow horses or "swinging a long loop," i.e., rustling.

shrinks with drying and makes a loose braid which is unsightly and not nearly as strong as a good tight braid.

Delbert tied the end of his strings in a knot, anchored it to a tree for something to pull against, soaped the first foot or so with a bar of soap dipped into warm water. The soap made the strings slip into the proper tightness easier. Always he braided some two or three inches back of where his strings actually crossed, pulling to about that distance above his work. The rope lay smooth and tight back of that, and he carefully pulled each string, wrapping it around his hand and laying it across his hip and leaning back on it until he had it the proper tension.

After the braiding was done, the rope got its first oil; it was thoroughly soaked with neatsfoot oil. Then he took a wrap around a tree and two men pulled it back and forth the complete length to smooth it. The longer it was used, the smoother it became, and the easier to throw. New, it kinked and tangled, but broken in it lay easy and handled sweet. Rain didn't affect it, it was braided too tightly to get wet. Manilla ropes, on the contrary, were like steel cables in wet weather.

A really fine braided rawhide rope was a status symbol par excellence! It took so much skill and labor to make one that few men could or would do it.

After we had been at the Roost a long time and Papa had more leisure, he figured out a way to twist rawhide into ropes. These were as much superior to the braided ones as the braided ones to the "seagrass" he could buy.

Being no novice with rawhide, nor unaware of a few simple principles of cordage, he knew he would have to twist the strings, run a space of them together, then turn them some more to keep the proper torsion for a tightly twisted rope. He tried a horsehair twisting machine, but it was too light for rawhide.

Finally he nailed up a plank between two posts of the saddle shed, bored four holes in it and installed twisters, made of long bolts, a hook on the outside and a handle on the inside of the plank. Fastening the strings to these hooks, he ran them out, being careful to keep them flat, and tied the outside end to a hair rope twirler. He inserted a cross made of quarter-inch bolts some 18 or 20 inches long, welded in the center, for a holder to keep the finished rope back so that he could keep running in twists in the strands, which were taken up as the rope itself twisted.

This was sort of a rough time for the crew; the rawhide had to be put together fast once he started, or it would get too dry to handle. Mama and we girls ran the twists in the strands, while he and the hired man put the rope together, the hired man holding the twirler out at the end of the strings while Papa went down each one as we carefully counted the turns on each crank to keep the twists even. He "ran" the strings down, letting them slide through his fingers, and where they were inclined to kink or pop inside out, he hand-twisted them into shape. He wanted the grain side of the rawhide on the outside all the way. When each string had been worked and all were twisting up smoothly, we ran in all the turns the strands would take without kinking.

Papa put his cross between the strands and pulled it back, holding the tension so that the hired man could run in the final twist of the rope with the hair twirler. This was about two or three feet for the first section. When the rope would take no more turns, we ran in some more twist at our end, Papa backed up some four or five feet, held the tension, and that much was made into final rope. After the first time, the rope unwound as Papa backed up, the strings running together, but loosely. This the hired man remedied with the twirler. The first few feet was difficult to get enough torsion worked down to the far end of the strings, but after that, it was a breeze and a rope ran together in just a few minutes.

The strings had to carry exactly the same number of turns, and he solved this by putting a "yoke" on the handles of the contrivance, so that one person could turn them and so that he was sure each strand was like all the others. The handles were modified a bit, too, so that they didn't bind against the plank.

For some reason, four-strand ropes tangled in use, so he made three-strand ropes almost exclusively. After they were broken in they were the best ropes in the world to throw and use. They never came untwisted, and they were really beautiful—real status symbols!

Breaking in a braided rope was not much of a job, but a twisted rope resisted like cable. Finally he bored three holes in the hitching rack post and threaded the ropes through these and pulled it back and forth attached to the saddle horn of one of us girls' mounts as long as he could get cooperation—and then a whole lot longer, as a rule! We also dragged them as we rode, I've dragged them for miles, the heavy honda catching on grass and brush and the rope whipping and writhing.

The hogstrings, after they were broken in, were really superb. They were light and not bulky, didn't slip, they were easy to handle, holding a good loop to snare the calf's feet, and they were easy to untie and come off the calf's front feet as the loop always sprang open. And they lasted two full seasons.

I made them for a few years when I was running the ranch, but somehow we just quit making them, and used sash-cord, which was perfectly satisfactory. It just wasn't quite as professional and fancy.

Papa often gave his handiwork away; many of his bits are still in use and perhaps there are some of his ropes in trunks somewhere. Ebb Gillies came along one time and Papa gave him a rope. Ebb was inordinately proud of it, but he used it.

These ropes handled so smoothly a man couldn't resist using one if he had it. And they made every other riders' eyes bug out in covetousness as the owner flaunted them on his saddle. Ebb hadn't had it very long when he laid it onto a bogged cow in the quicksand of the San Rafael, gave a mighty heave and "stranded" his beautiful rope.

Ebb was a Mormon and no cusser. But the situation demanded some release of feeling. He jumped off his horse, felt the ruined rope, slammed his hat down on the ground and jumped on it with both boots and said:

"Some people wonder why I'm baldheaded! The reason is I got so mad on this boggy river, I *pulled* it all out. I'm only sorry now I can't start all over again."

Papa (and all the rest of us) really loved working with rawhide, but Mama was somewhat unfriendly to it. One time she was washing dishes and Papa was braiding a hackamore noseband. He came over, tested the dishwater with his finger while she moved aside and watched. When he gathered up his strings to wet them in her dishpan she said, "Oh, no you don't!"

He paused and looked at her in surprise. "I felt it, and it's not too hot, it won't hurt my strings."

"But those dirty strings won't do my dishes any good. Nothing doing!" And Mama moved around to protect her domain.

As he prepared a bucket of warm water, he marvelled at the unreasonableness of women. After all his care in keeping those strings clean, he just didn't understand her!

My father originated the technique of making hatbands out of rings, using horsehair. He watched my mother tatting and opined that you could do the same thing with horeshair. My mother was skeptical, but he looked at the tatting and said it could be done. By wrapping the horsehair around a stick, then throwing halfhitches on it like tatting, it would work;

he knew it would. It was fun to do something new and we set out, all of us, to perfect his idea. And it did work, beautifully, but we learned several little tricks about it.

Procuring long horsehair was no problem; we never did trim our horses' tails unless they got burs or witch knots. Their graceful, swinging tails as they moved around working cattle are among my most cherished memories. All this long hair was handy when it came to working horsehair, and we found that it was tough and pliable. The hair from mares' tails was not strong, it was brittle, deteriorated by the urine. However, this was no problem, we never rode mares and the hair we used came from the nearest horse.

Horsehair rope has been in use in the cow country forever, the joke being that it was made in the penitentiaries and the men who were expert were suspected of having learned it there. Some of them did.

Dafton Thompson* tells that's where one of the Swasey's had learned it. One afternoon while Swasey ran out a beautiful set of strings a returned Mormon missionary watched him and bragged about his exploits in the mission field. Finally the missionary asked Swasey where he had learned to do this work.

"Oh," Swasey replied modestly, "I just picked it up on my mission."

For this craft of rope making, horsehair from broncs whose tails were always "pulled" as a safety measure, since the long hair might get caught on spurs or equipment, or trimmings from manes and tails were saved until we had a couple of

---

*Dafton was raised by his uncle, Henry Thompson, and didn't use his name of Christenson until his marriage and move to Salt Lake City. When he was a young bronc stomper, he worked for Preston Nutter, one of the leading cattlemen of the West. Nutter liked him (everyone liked Dafton), and when one of the broncs laid him up with disabling bruises and contusions, Nutter put him to driving his car, and Dafton enjoyed a couple of months of that plush assignment. Nutter could never remember "Dafton" and called him De Luxe. To this day, old cowhands on the Arizona Strip know him only as D'luxe Thompson.

gunnysacks of various colors all mixed up. Then, one spring day, a fellow sat down on the sunny side of a building, spread a tarp and started to "pick" the horsehair, laying it almost strand by strand every-which-way until he had a mat some two feet across and about two inches thick in the middle. He then rolled this up carefully, and when he had several rolls, got someone to whirl his twirler and started running out strings.

This twirler was a piece of wood about fourteen inches long by about two inches thick and maybe a bit wider than that. It was whittled tapering to one end, where a hole was bored about two and a half inches back from the end. This end was then shaped into a small neck and a knob with the hole back of them.

To use, a pin about four inches long, also wood, was whittled with a knob on the end; this was run through the hole in the twirler. Fashioning a loop of the horsehair in one of the rolled mats, the fellow slipped it over the knob of the twirler, his helper whirled the club-like twirler around and around on the pin, the heavy end making it easy to twirl. As he twisted up the string, the fellow played out the horsehair from the roll, pulling it into a neat line.

When they had a string the required length, they made another, and when they had three or four, depending on what they were going to use it for (cinches were two-strand), they twisted them all tightly and "ran" them together for the finished rope. We made our cinches of horsehair in the early days, but my father didn't do much of this as he got older, and now nylon is easy to get and just as good.

Another method of making horsehair articles in the penitentiary where time was no item was to make a bunch of strings, tie them (about 20) around a sashcord or other round "core" and starting with a twine string, half hitch each string over it while wrapping it around the cord. This made an even, beautiful round rope which was used for fancy headstalls, I understand. I have made it, but it is slow, the horsehair doesn't wear long enough to justify the time involved, and it is not showy enough for hatbands, which is what we started out to make.

Horsehair could be braided or plaited, too, and hatbands were made that way, using strings of different colors to create diamond-shaped patterns. To make strings of horsehair that would stay together like a cord or thread, we selected ten to twenty hairs, depending on how many strands we were going to use and how thick we wanted the finished braid. We laid the ends of the longest hairs we could get together and tied a knot in the end which had been pulled from the horse's tail. We split the hairs into two strands, holding them apart in the left hand with the first finger between them, just below the knot. With our right thumb and finger we grasped the knot and started turning it, pulling the string out as we laid in twists until we reached the other end, in which we tied another knot. This strand stayed twisted into one string as long as the ends were not untied.

The simplest braid was five flat. Tie the ends of five strands together after making each one of a counted number of hairs. Divide the strands into two on the left side and three on the right and cross the two center strands, the two-string on top. Take the outside string of the right side, wind it under the middle strand and over the crossed strand. This makes three strands on the left; now, take the outside left string, bring it under the middle one and over the string just brought over from the outside of the right-hand side. This same *modus operandi* is used for any odd-number of strings.

These hatbands are pretty, and I see them from time to time, but they are nothing like the beautiful ring hatbands my father developed. The rings are about an inch in diameter, with bars through them, and fastened together in various ways, usually with small rings. They are difficult and time-consuming, but the result is worth the effort.

We chose seven hairs, picking the longest hairs from a lock cut or pulled from the tail of the best endowed horse in the outfit. These we pulled carefully from the lock so as not to tangle the rest of the hair, then threaded the butt end (end next to the horse) into an embroidery needle. My fancy-working mother always had plenty of these on hand. We divided the strand and ran it together as for braiding. The bottom end would be held together by the work, of course, but the top half we hitched over the needle, pulling the knot back onto the strand, making it as small as possible but one that would hold.

This strand we then ran through our mouth to moisten it. We tried everything to moisten and give the horsehair a little elasticity and "dressing" so it would pull down into the stitches tightly, but nothing worked as well as just plain spit. It was our belief that if a person was too fancy to taste horsehair, he was too fastidious to punch cows in the first place.

The only other tool besides the needle that we used was a stick to wrap the ring on. This began as a tapered round stick about eight inches long with a groove lengthwise under where the ring was wrapped, and just above this point the stick was whittled about half in two so that the needle could be grasped and pulled up when it was shoved along the groove under the wrapped horsehair. This was later simplified by cutting the groove spirally around the stick. I later changed this by cutting the stick to about three inches long so that it fit into my palm and the strand of horsehair didn't snag on it.

I may be superstitious but I think the best wood for this stick is a round piece of piñon limb, long dead so that the bark has all weathered off. I whittle this to a tapered form, cut a groove around it and I am ready for business. No other wood seems to hold the horsehair together as well, or to "age" into perfect aesthetic use as does this section of a piñon limb, and the longer I use one the more I like it.

Around this form the horsehair is wrapped until about 30 strands, individual strands, of horsehair are wrapped tightly. This can vary, but each ring should contain the same number of hairs. Usually I wrap with a couple of extra hairs and hold the ends with my thumb while I take a couple of wraps with the needle strand (we considered hair shorter than 30 inches not worth bothering with), then take the first half-hitch on the ring, pulling it down about ⅛ inch back of the groove. The next stitch is made in the opposite direction, making a single "over and under" as in tatting. At least half the ring is worked before it is slipped off the stick.

The way to tell how to take the next stitch is to note which side the strand comes out of the last stitch, then put the needle through the groove with the point aimed in that same direction. That will turn the stitch the opposite or right way. If the ring is formed of alternately directed stitches, the work lies flat. In making bars in the rings, we thought they were more attractive if made of half-hitches turned the same way each time, which wrapped a ridge around and around the basic bar.

When the ring is filled with stitches, the knot is released from the needle, and after the ring is soaked in the mouth again, the needle is threaded back through five or six stitches, sewing through the half-hitches as inconspicuously as possible. Horsehair never slips if put together tightly when moist. It never loses its "kink" and never ravels back.

Hatband rings are about an inch across, and it takes about 20 rings, depending on their size and the size of the hat. Allow for the bows and tie, making the band about two inches shorter than the circumference of the hat crown.

Rings may be fastened together in a number of ways. The simplest is to make the next ring through the last one by holding it against the bottom of the stick as the ring is wrapped.

When finished, the length of rings is twisted until all of them lie flat. I sew it to a strip of cardboard to keep it flat while I apply the bows and tie.

The most ornate looking hatbands are those with bars in the rings, and smaller rings over these holding the larger rings together. These will lie flat enough to handle without sewing to cardboard.

To make the bow and tie, braid two strings about eight inches long, four strand round, finishing the ends with tassles. Select shorter hair and wrap a few strands around your first three fingers of your left hand to make a circle, which you hold together by wrapping the last couple of turns around and around the other hairs. What you are aiming for is a circle of horsehair about two inches across, that you can handle without its falling apart. Slip two strands of your braided tie through this ring and with the other two strings of the braid, tie into half a square knot, pulling the ring up against the braiding tightly. Pull the ring down with these ends for the tassle. Wrap just fairly snugly below the knot with about ten or fifteen wraps of a separate two horsehairs. With a needle threaded with not more than four hairs, start covering this knot by working half-hitches over this wrapped string tie, and going around and around, letting the stitches gradually build back over the unsightly knot. To me, this is the real drudgery of the whole operation, and the hardest to make look smooth and workmanlike.

Cut and trim the tassle—remembering that you can always cut a little more off if you want to. Turn the string around and undo the loose braiding at the beginning end, and put it in tightly, then apply a tassle to that end. Make two of these strings.

Fasten these strings, one to each end of your hatband, leaving a short end about two inches long, running a loop through the ring then the ends through it so that you have a double half-hitch over the end ring with the ends going toward the back of the work.

Cross these strings, the long ends on top, and bring them back leaving loops on each side of the center knot for bows, with the tassle of the short end of each string and that of the long end of the opposite side together. This makes six strands in the center which you are holding with your left thumb and finger. Work a small ring around these, with five hairs in a needle, using about five or six wraps around the strands. Put on just enough stitches on this holding ring to make it lie flat along the strands. Put in another ring with the stitches lying the opposite direction, and then a center ring, with the stitches standing up. All this is pretty difficult, but you want three little rings, rather snug, around all the strands of the ties. In working these holding rings, I catch one strand of one of the ties to hold them in place, letting the other strands slip to pull the hatband down tightly on the hat. This does not hold very well; the band must be sewed to the hat in several places.

To make the hatband lie flat and look well, it is a good idea when finished to steam it carefully with an iron through a wet cloth until it lies flat, then slip it on a hat or a cardboard circle to dry.

Making one of these hatbands is an awful job, but there is just nothing quite so beautiful. When my nephew, AC Ekker, won the National Intercollegiate All-Around Rodeo title, there was nothing I could do to show how proud of him I was but to make him a hatband. I sent to him for some horsehair, and he produced both black and white of the required length. I made both him and his father the old traditional hatbands, that had not been seen at the Roost for thirty years. It took almost 150 hours of work for each one.

And now they do not wear them, keep them hanging up at home because they are far too valuable and beautiful to take a chance on losing them. Oh, well, I tried.

My father on Kazan, one of his favorite horses.

14

We Built a Ranch

IN 1925 MY FATHER decided that his range was far overstocked—not for feed but for water; a bad year and his springs would fall off, and he could lose half he owned in a week. For the past three or four years he had never let the Roost Spring go longer than a week during the summer without checking it. Most of his cattle ranged there, and if something happened to the spring—if even one cow got over the fence and tramped out the headbox and V-trough so that the water wasted down the canyon, he could lose more than he cared to imagine. Besides, the thought of choking cattle sickened him; he had had enough of that always when the pond at the cabin dried up and he had to close the gate and force the cattle to trail to the Roost for water. If there should come a time when there was just no water anywhere— he was haunted by that.

The year of 1925 he gathered and trailed out to market over a thousand head of cattle. I know, because I helped him do it. This left a comfortable herd on the range, which had increased to about six or seven hundred head when the estate was settled in 1928.

During the winter of 1927-28, there just was not much to do. The cattle left on the range could fend for themselves, and my father had no building project for the winter. He had built "the little cabin" for a bedroom the winter before, and he spent the cold months mostly lying on the bed out there. He was sick, but in the years since, I have begun to wonder if he wasn't more at loose ends than physically ill. I spent most of the winter there with Joe, who was a year old that winter, and Mama was gone quite a bit. Hazel was in school at St. Marys of the Wasatch, and Mama visited her several times.

In the spring, Mama coaxed him into going to Salt Lake City to see a doctor. They rather enjoyed the trip; they went to shows, dined with the Coles who were good friends as Cole had been the banker in Green River and had liked this rough frontiersman.

In the hospital, Papa was most unhappy, but he did get his tonsils out—many years too late. If this had been done when he was young, it would have saved all those terrible bouts with quinsey. When he got out of the hospital, he and Mama picked up a truck he was buying for my husband, and they started home.

When they got to Castle Gate, where his sister lived, he was just too sick to go on. Aunt Olive and her family were moving to a ranch at Roosevelt, with most of their furniture already gone, but Papa and Mama could get by with rather meager furniture for a day or two until he got well enough to go on the other 75 miles to Green River.

On June 16, 1928, he died early in the morning, from complications following his tonsilectomy.

And what of the Roost? It is still a good cow outfit, owned by Arthur and managed by him and his son AC, who is married and has two small children.

Being open range with only a few school sections, the

Roost is today under the rule of Bureau of Land Management. The main waters had been developed by my father and the springs that he put into troughs are still running into those same wooden troughs after fifty years. Arthur has put in one more trough at the Roost, but other than that the range has been kept in good condition by the usual trail maintenance and corral repair and cleaning the springs from time to time.

When my father sold his cattle down in 1925, he was afraid of what a drought could do to him, and he was farseeing. The west has suffered a drought cycle from almost that time, with but a few years when enough precipitation fell to bring good feed. All the western ranges are depleted. The Roost has suffered, too, although the dry years have kept water from the ponds the BLM has made there, so that there has been no overstocking.

It has been a major problem for the BLM to use the money that should go back onto the range. The system is that instead of reducing fees, the promise is made to spend some of the grazing fee directly on range improvement to the area from which it was produced. One of their money-using projects was a fence across the head of Antelope, from the head of the Roost Canyon to the Horseshoe, some ten or twelve miles. Probably not more than twenty head of cattle of either Moores at North Springs or Arthur Ekker at the Roost drifted onto the other man's range—and no one cared if they did. It was never a problem. The Bureau of Land Management had decided to fence between permittees, so they constructed this drift fence, which was blown under by sand dunes in some places before it was finished. Sand was all that ever did drift there, and this "drift fence" didn't do much to control that, either.

In the days of my childhood that I have been recalling, only a few cowpunchers, chuck-line riders, sheepherders, oil-diggers and prospectors crossed the undulating grassy Roost

Flats and dropped over the ridge onto the lovely Twin Corrals country, but today so many people want to see the beauties of the canyons, buttes, mesas and ridges of that area so rich in geology and history, that Arthur and AC have had to become part-time dude wranglers. They call their enterprise Outlaw Trails, and no man comes back from a trip into the deep recesses of the Maze or the inner gorge of the Colorado River without a lasting memory of the experience. The beauty and grandeur settle into his spirit and remain a sweetness savored for the rest of his life.

To us who lived there, it is a glory in our hearts that can never die. It has been a privilege to record at least some of it!

My Father, Mother, and the old Ford truck, Betsy, that was called "Ship of the Desert" because it was equipped with auxiliary gears and could travel over the sand.

Afterword

What happened to the rest of us after, Papa, the king, was dead—
I met Big Henry Dusserre on the street that morning. When he asked
me how Papa was and I told him he was gone, Big Henry put his
work-worn hands over his face and burst into tears, so great was his
love and admiration for my father.

The next year or two was filled with settling the estate, branding
the cattle over to us three survivors, with Mama leasing hers and
Hazel's to Art Murry to be trailed across the Green River to the Big
Flats country near what is now Dead Horse Point.

In 1929, when my husband, Mel Marsing, and I signed the
papers to buy the range rights from Mama and Hazel, he was lame,
having been hit on the thigh by a knot in a rope of a horse he was
leading. Two months later, on September 13, 1929, he was dead of
blood poisoning from this injury, and I was left with two little boys—
Jack had been born September 30, 1928—and a cow outfit.

I ran the outfit for a few years during the blackest of the Depression, then married again and sold to Arthur and Hazel and moved
to Oregon. There my husband and I separated and I was faced with
raising not two, but three little boys. Noel was four years old.

Noel grew up to do the thing I most wanted to do. He joined
the Air Force and after being a jet pilot instructor in fighters, is now
on assignment in Germany.

Joe grew up to be a fine heavy-equipment operator on highway
building, and there are few roads in southeastern Utah that have not

seen his handiwork. Jack passed the Civil Service examination for mine inspectors with the highest grade in the state of Utah. I am very proud of this, he has an eighth grade education, but is a long way from stupid. He is just entering a new career.

Arthur and Hazel were very successful at the Roost. At the peak of this success, Hazel died of emphysema in January, 1969. In the spring of 1970, Arthur married Lela Wilcox Anderson, which pleased us all greatly. She was a girlhood friend of Hazel's and mine, and from one of the oldest cattle families in the country. Her family is raised, too, and she and Arthur have found a great deal of companionship and fun in building a life for themselves in their late years.

Arthur and Hazel had four children. Eddyjo, the oldest son, is an investment consultant in Caiifornia; AC, the youngest of the family, is associated with his father at the Roost, after a successful rodeo career, and runs river and jeep trips with his Outlaw Trails. Gaye, the youngest daughter, has her own dancing studio in Cedar City, and in the spring of 1971, Evelyn (Tissy) the older daughter, was mother of three queens. She has three daughters, the youngest was Valentine Queen of her elementary school; the oldest was queen of the University of Utah engineering school, while Sharon realized every 17-year-old's dream by being Prom Queen of her school, Skyline High School in Salt Lake City.

In 1970 the CowBelles of Utah honored my mother on her 86th birthday as being a woman of the state contributing significantly to the cattle industry of Utah. It was well earned; there never would have been a ranch at the Roost if she hadn't lived right out on the range winter and summer. Mama was not much impressed, but the rest of us were!

And I am well started on a writing career.

You could say that we Robbers Roosters have made our marks in the world, and we all think it is because we had a different heritage. We had learned to hit things another lick, and we had wider vision than other people.

The people we grew up with have found their niches, too; most of them are successful and people of substance. The Chaffin boys, Ken, Clell and Fawn, became men of some property, and the Tidwell boys, Leland and Delbert, own ranches in Green River.

Hazel, Arthur, Eddyjo, and Tissy in front of their house at Doobinky just before they bought the Roost and moved there.

Noel (two) sitting on a calf's head while I brand it.

Joe and Jack, about seven and five years old, but real cow hands. Note their lariats; they were equipped.

A. C. Ekker, who now owns and manages the Roost, with the trophies and saddle awards from the National Collegiate Rodeo, which he won at St. George in 1967.